To Maryangela Roman,
In appreciation for your
interest in my work.
Audrey Mettel Fixmer 9/14/96

Grand Mom

Growing Old Gracefully
& OTHER LIKELY STORIES

by
Audrey Mettel Fixmer

**Published by
Write-On-Time Publishing**

Individual columns in this book first appeared in
The Catholic Herald, Madison, Wisconsin.
They are reprinted here with permission of
The Catholic Herald. Other works first appeared in
The Catholic Twin Circle, published in
Los Angeles, California, and
Our Family Magazine, published in
Battleford, Saskatchewan, Canada

Published by Write-On-Time Publishing
Post Office Box 216
Fort Atkinson, WI 53538

Manufactured in the United States of America
Typesetting by Estelle Wiesmann,
Protype Service, Fort Atkinson, Wisconsin
Cover Design by Rhonda Neuenfeldt,
New Field Designs, Deerfield, Wisconsin

ISBN 0-9642672-0-9

First Edition

This book
is dedicated to my
Sounding Board, Bob,
who laughs if it's funny, cries if it's touching,
snores if it's boring.
So I know
whether to print it or toss it,
so you'll either read it or never run across it!

ACKNOWLEDGEMENTS

I am indebted to Mary Uhler, the editor of *The Catholic Herald*, for encouraging me to write my Grand Mom column, and to my readers, who write or stop me at church to say they find my columns funny, touching, or inspirational.

I am also grateful to my funny family and friends, who inspire me with their wit and laugh at mine, especially Pat Opatz, Mary McBride, and all the Funny Fixmers: Bob and my Krazy Kids Rob, Tom, Tim, Elizabeth, Kathy, Kris, Gretchen, Patty, John, and Mark. (It was Kris who asked if my hearing aid battery was dead one day when I failed to laugh at her jokes.) Thanks to Estelle, Rhonda, and JoAnn for their production help, and to Fr. Duane and the Communion Breakfast Club for cheering me on.

All those wonderful people who invite me to speak at their banquets and luncheons are helping me keep alive the myth that I have something worthwhile to say, and that growing old gracefully might still be possible if we can just keep the joints oiled and the brain clear. . .and a fresh supply of batteries.

TABLE OF CONTENTS

AREN'T WE GRAND?

I've done a lot of things in my 66 years that have brought me joy and satisfaction Leading the list, without a doubt, is capturing my husband, Bob, on the rebound from a Benedictine seminary, and bringing eleven souls into this world: one saint and ten little devils who are still working to elevate their status. Earning my college degrees with ten children at home was as gratifying as it was hectic, as was becoming a teacher with an additional 135 kids to worry about. None of that seems surprising, however. What did take me by surprise was the satisfaction I have found in writing my Grand Mom column for the senior pages of *The Catholic Herald*.

Since my retirement from teaching in 1990, I have jumped off the treadmill and taken time to stop and smell the coffee. In fact, as I write my column, I see my readers as neighbors who have dropped by to share a cup of coffee and a few laughs with me. We enjoy philosophizing about the crazy state of the world today, celebrating the achievements of modern technology, reminiscing about how it was, wisecracking about how it is, sharing the news from the front lines where our grandchildren are dodging bullets, and delighting in God's humor.

In fact, it was my acknowledgment of God's humor which led me to insist on the Grand Mom title. I had to do something to distinguish myself from my grandmother, who wore her religion like a black shroud. In the thirty or more years that I knew her, I do not recall ever hearing Grandmother laugh aloud or show approval of anything we kids said or did. She wore spotless Hoover aprons in her kitchen, but dressed only in black when she left the house. But then, funerals were her only social pastime, as far as I knew.

In the 1950s when Grandmother heard her two middle-aged daughters laughing over an episode of "I Love Lucy," she scolded them with a shake of her head, a sad "Tsk, tsk!" and the rhetorical question, "Would the Blessed Mother laugh!"

When Mother told me this, I shouted, "Heck, yes! She sure would!"

Grandmother was still in her own home when I took Bob there for the first time. He was greatly amused at the decor of her bathroom, to which I had become immune over the years. From a seated position one was treated to a large picture of a sad-eyed Sacred Heart of Jesus, looking down with compassion from the opposite wall. A holy water fount was conveniently located next to the door. Bob wondered aloud if one was supposed to say a prayer of petition going in and a prayer of thanksgiving upon leaving. And was there a danger of a loss of faith for those unfortunate souls who did not meet with success?

Grandma was the title for my mother and Bob's mother as our kids were growing up. They were admirable women, both of them, but restricted in so many ways that I find it equally difficult to identify with them. They never worked outside the home, where they wore cotton house-dresses and baked cakes from scratch, boiled water for the laundry, and slaved over stoves and ironing boards. They wore silk floral print dresses for church on Sunday, and sensible shoes always. And their bodies were held rigid by corsets with bones! Their husbands dictated how they should vote and what they should cook for supper.

I never did wear those dreadful bony corsets, and I tossed out my last girdle 20 years ago. Now I wear tee shirts, jeans and sneakers at home, fashionable clothes for dress, and tell my husband to throw something into the microwave if I'm not back from my aerobics class on time. Is it any wonder I can't answer to "Grandma" either?

As our kids were growing up I was always Mom, as in "Mom, what's for supper?" and "Mom, you didn't really tell my teacher that, did you?" The Catholic women of my generation are the big guns of the baby boom and a vanishing breed, because today's moms can't produce the quantities of children that we did and still hold down full-time jobs. So now that we have arrived at the exalted state of grand motherhood, it seems entirely appropriate that we be referred to as Grand Moms.

Bob tells me it's lucky for me that our language has adopted the French *grande* as opposed to the German word, *grosse*. I say call me gross and you won't get anything for dinner!

Ours is the Grand as in "Grand Canyon". . . awesome! Grand as in "Grand Hotel". . . always room for one more. It's Grand as in "Grande Dame," a great lady of certain age and dignity, and it's the Grand in "Grand Slam," taking all the tricks, since we mastered many tricks along the way. But mostly it's the Grand in "Grandstand," where the view is best, the perspective great.

So that is what I try to do in my Grand Mom columns. I share my stories and tricks for survival, (like finding God's humor in the most unlikely places), view the parade passing by from my grandstand seat of seniority, and just enjoy. In the words of the song, "On a clear day you can see forever!"

So pour yourself a cup of coffee, and pull up a chair. There's always room for one more at my table.

MEET
THE KIDS

WE EARNED IT

The name "Granny" evokes an image of that feisty little ball of fire that darted around our television sets back in the sixties, Al Capp's Lil' Abner character, smoking a corn cob pipe. "Grandma," on the other hand, calls to mind our own ancestors in their house dresses and starched aprons, masters of the bottomless cookie jar and the perpetual-motion rocking chair. Neither of those monikers fits today's grandmothers, and I, for one, wish to go on record as demanding a more fitting title, one that suggests the dignity and unique position we hold today. "Grand Mom" ought to do it.

I'm referring particularly to that special breed of silver-haired ladies who were the Big Guns of the baby boomers, the Catholic moms of the '50s and '60s. We are the Veterans of the

Great Rhythm Wars, an Endangered Species. Today we blend in nicely with other ladies our age, but we can all recall when we stood out from our Protestant counterparts like a Roman collar in a topless bar.

Just walking down the street, you knew the difference. The Protestant moms were the ones flashing by in their shiny station wagons, transporting their 2.3 children to a ballet class or violin lesson. We Catholic moms were the waddling walruses, trudging along pulling a coaster wagon containing a bag of groceries and the two-year-old holding the baby, while the three and four-year-olds dragged behind. And we had number five in the hopper.

The Protestant moms could sing in their church choirs or stroll down the aisle in their Easter finery. We Catholic moms were sentenced to 20 years in the crying room.

In the O.B. wards they were welcomed with a brass band and showered with candy, flowers, and cute little pink and blue things. When we Catholic moms arrived, the nurses whispered, "It's her again!"

They could always get a loan for a new camper, a cruise, or a divorce, but that same banker would hide when he saw Catholic moms coming. That's when I learned the real meaning of FDIC (Fertile Dames Impossible Credit).

They were the gardeners with manicured lawns and designer garbage; we grew swing sets, trikes, popsicle sticks, and wheels-off-things.

They were the loving wives who greeted their husbands each evening with a pitcher of martinis and a romantic dinner by candlelight. We snapped, "Don't kiss me, you fool! Check the calendar!"

The calendar! We were obsessed with it, trying to make the darn Rhythm Method work. Oh, we knew how it was supposed to work, all right. Find the center day between periods. That's ovulation. Cross it out with a big X and then cross out four days before and four days after to abstain. Each time another baby is born, cross out an additional two or three days on either side until you've blocked out weeks. Then pray that someone invents a bedroom calendar that glows in the dark, and when it reads "ovulation!" it sends out rays that turn your body into an electric fence (temporarily, of course).

That was the Church's bootcamp for sainthood. We graduated from that and went on to fight the Battle of the Bulge, first with Playtex Eighteen Hour girdles (plus two hours to shove it all in and a half hour to peel it off, another day shot!) and later under Jane Fonda's command we huffed and puffed but never did blow that flab away.

Then we fought the Battle of the Larder. Each fall we snared every beautiful tomato and bean we could capture and imprisoned them into glass jars and freezers so that come winter we could produce gallons of goulash to eat with the fifteen loaves of bread we baked each week.

The Battle of the Garments dragged on for years! I had nightmares of suffocating at the bottom of a clothes chute, as thousands of little socks, shirts, pants, jackets, sheets, and diapers dropped upon me, finally muffling my screams. Would I be hailed as the first hero to die on that battlefield? Not a chance!

The truth of the matter is that society paid us the same kind of respect that they did the Vietnam Vets. "So you survived all that? That's nice." I kept waiting for the Vatican to erect a monument to the Veterans of the great Rhythm Wars, or at least to establish the Golden Ovary Award, but nooooo!

It's okay though. We have reaped our own rewards. No longer must we rush out of daily Mass after communion. We have time to stop and chat with parishioners in our exclusive silver-haired group, and sometimes gather at a local tea room for a cup of coffee. The church is like our kids. For years we thought they made unreasonable demands, but now that we are at an age when some suffer from loneliness, we find in them our greatest joy, a kind of social security as well as spiritual security.

We delight in our children's parenting skills as they juggle careers and family. We love spending time with our grandchildren, a joy we missed with our own. And we don't mind the responsibility of occasional baby-sitting when we can fit it in between our volunteer work, bridge games, luncheons, or our season tickets with various theater groups.

We don't smoke corncob pipes like the Al Capp's Grannie did; we don't wear housedresses and starched aprons and reign over the bottomless cookie jar like Grandma did. Ours is the sweat-suit and the Reeboks, the Senior Discounted dining and travel itineraries, and Elder Hostel course offerings. Old Rocking Chair must wait; we carry membership cards to health clubs and credit cards for airline connections to our children across the nation.

We got the title "Grand Mom" the hard way. We earned it.

MOTHERHOOD, CATHOLIC STYLE

I 'll say this for motherhood, Catholic style—it can't be beat as a training ground for sainthood. I'm not talking here about just getting inside the pearly gates. Following the ten commandments ought to do that. But to play in the Big Leagues, you've got to be working on the more advanced course: Corporal Works of Mercy and Spiritual Works of Mercy. These are the Church's gourmet recipes for sanctity. And what better training ground could you find than motherhood, Catholic style, the way we experienced it back in the '50s and '60s?

Take the Spiritual Works of Mercy. Remember those? Like "Instruct the ignorant." Heck, we did that every day. "No, sweetheart, Mommy will wash the dishes. You don't have to lick the plate."

Or "Counsel the doubtful." Good one. "Of course God loves you, son. He's not nearly so disgusted with that long hair as I am. Look how he wore His!"

"Admonish the sinner." That was my specialty. "Okay, for putting your little sister in the clothes dryer, you are going to wash the dishes every night for a week and clean the peanut butter off the kitchen ceiling."

"Bear wrongs patiently." That could be tough. I remember a well meaning neighbor saying, "I can understand ignorant people having so many children, but you two are well educated. Why would you have more children than you can afford to educate?" What do you say? We were well educated in Catholic schools, Ma'am?

If the Spiritual Works were hard, they were nothing compared to the Corporal Works! "Shelter the Homeless" Sure! And the Overnights and the Bedwetters and the Fugitives from Justice! We got 'em all. Along with our "goodnights" we had the standard question, "Do your parents know where you are? And in which bed will I find you if they call?"

"Feed the Hungry." Oh, good Lord, did I feed the hungry! And it started out so innocently. We were living in a trailer in University Village, where Bob was in graduate school, and I fixed two pork chops for our dinner. Our oldest, Robbie, was cutting teeth, so after removing the meat I handed my bone to him in the high chair. He glared at the bone, slammed it on the floor, pointed to my plate and demanded, "Meat!" (It was his first word—not Mama or Dada—but meat!) I suddenly caught a glimpse of what lay ahead. And thinking of buying three pork chops instead of two, I made what was, perhaps, the understatement of my life. I said, "This is going to be expensive!"

Little did I dream that down the line it would take twelve pork chops, five pounds of potatoes, twenty-four ears of sweet corn, a gallon of milk, two loaves of bread, a sheet cake and two quarts of peaches to feed the Lord's masses. How I wished that original Frugal Gourmet would appear on television to teach us how to multiply loaves and fishes!

I baked six loaves of bread three times a week and bought ten loaves for lunches. When I packed lunches I used an assembly line method: deal out one loaf in single file, slather the margarine over with a wide spatula, slap on a pound of bologna slices, deal out another loaf for the tops. I was secretly proud that my teenage boys demanded three sandwiches apiece. (Proof that they were growing fast and would soon leave home.) It wasn't until just a few years ago that I learned they didn't really eat all those sandwiches. They traded some for Twinkies, and sold others to buy cigarettes!

But the worst of those Corporal Works was that darn "Clothe the Naked." Every last one of those little buggers came into this world stark naked, and demanded changing every few minutes. I once figured that by the time they left home they had gone through approximately 500 pairs of jeans, 720 undershirts, 730 underpants, 900 shirts, 700 shoes and 10,000 socks, give or take a thou. When the grandparents came to visit we played this little game called, "Match the socks." I'd bring out this big bushel basket of unmated socks (in a big family kids' socks go through more divorces than Hollywood stars), and the grandparents would be kept busy all afternoon. A prize awaited the one who could match the most socks, something wonderful to wear to dinner that night: a set of earplugs.

Despite the Church's mandate to "Clothe the naked," I soon realized it was sending mixed messages. This occurred to me one Sunday morning at church after a particularly hectic departure. Robbie was late returning from his paper route, Tommy and Timmy were fighting over a donut one minute and the comics the next. Patty's bottle had boiled over and needed cooling, so I yelled to Mary Beth to take care of that when she finished dressing Krissy. Then I ran upstairs to dress two-year-old Gretchen and was horrified to find clothing blown about the room as they tried on every dress and can-can petticoat they could find. And Gretchen's drawer, like her bottom, was bare. That meant running clear to the basement for clean underwear, but meanwhile, I could put her dress on right here.

So with a pink ruffled Gretchen perched on one hip, I raced down the stairs to hear the phone ringing crazily off the wall, and Bob tooting the horn in the driveway. When I arrived in the basement laundry room, I stood there repeating, "Now what did I come down here for?" Another blast of the horn reminded me that Mass started in five minutes, so whatever it was must wait.

Of course, we were so late that we had to parade clear to the front. And Father was already in the pulpit reading that dreadful thing about not being so concerned with material things. We filed into the first available pew, second from the front, and just as I sat down, Gretchen leaned over the pew to retrieve her doll, and suddenly I remembered what I went to the laundry room for. Her panties!

I pinned her to the seat with my arm, just as Father was emoting, "Consider the lilies of the field! They neither spin nor weave. Yet Solomon in all his glory was not arrayed as one of these!". . .and I thought, "I should have raised lilies!"

GUARDIAN ANGELS. . .
I DO BELIEVE!

As a senior at Madonna High School, I could spout off the Five Proofs for the Existence of God According to Thomas Aquinas. That was a long time ago, and I've forgotten most of them. I can still, however, offer Ten Proofs for the Existence of Guardian Angels According to Fixmer Phenomenon.

Like all young parents, we were nervous about protecting our little ones from falls that would maim or freak accidents that could kill. We read warning labels and Dr. Spock, listened to experienced parents, and boned up on child psychology. That satisfied us with the first child. But when the second baby came along, diluting our protective powers, we became more edgy. With the third (all in diapers) it was Fixmer Frenzy 'round the clock. We couldn't afford a mother's helper, much less a nanny. What to do?

Guardian Angels to the rescue! As we knelt with our eldest son, Rob, beside his bed each night, the prayer we said together not only served to give our son a spiritual companion, but it lifted an immense burden from our shoulders as well:

> Angel of God, my Guardian Dear,
> To whom His love commits me here,
> Ever this day be at my side
> To light and guard; to rule and guide. Amen

With numbers four and five we prayed, "Thanks for the blessings, but enough already!" Like the insistent host who gushes, "You like that? Here have some more," He ignored our subtle protests. So when six and seven came along, our prayers had a little edge: "Nice that you pour out your love on us, but quit drowning us, will you, please?"

Our eighth child was retarded, but Patty was so sweet that we prayed, "Okay, we can handle even this. . .as long as it's *the end*." As a friend of a friend said, "It's a good thing the Church didn't allow The Pill because I would have overdosed for sure."

But it didn't, so I didn't. And numbers nine and ten came along. "If this is the way you treat your friends, Lord, no wonder you have so few," I grumbled in the words of St. Therese. Then I added my own. "And since this is your idea, not mine, you can take responsibility for them."

And did He ever! He sent out His all-star-team of G.A.s to work 'round the clock in all the spots that parents couldn't cover. Good thing these G.A.s were spirits. If they had required space, laundry, and meals, I might have evicted them before they had a chance to prove their worth.

Here then are my "Ten Proofs for the Existence of Guardian Angels":

1. Mark, the youngest, had poor vision and walked right off the roof of the sun-deck, breaking a leg just six months after breaking an arm springing off a bed. We were sure he would grow up crooked, but he straightened out and developed a beautiful, muscular body. Thanks, G.A.!

2. John, on a dare, rode his bike under a swinging swing. He was hospitalized with a concussion, and we feared permanent brain damage, but he graduated last week from the University and is accepted into law school. So thanks, G.A.!

3. Patty, though retarded, outsmarted everyone with her determination to succeed. She is totally independent, self-supporting, and happily married. Thanks, G.A.!

4. Gretchen, who was our only child to be trusted with a car in high school, showed amazing maturity and skill in chauffeuring the younger kids when I went to work. Thanks, G.A.!

5. Kris, always in a hurry to go places, used to slide down the stairs on her belly when she was too small to walk down them, and an attempt to ride a broom handle at age five put her into the hospital. We feared she might never have children after that, but today she has three beautiful daughters. Thanks, G.A.!

6. Kathi, a passenger in my overcrowded car as I drove to St. Joseph School, flew out the door as I rounded the last corner, but sprang to her feet, and chased behind us, shouting indignantly, "Wait for me!" Now she helps other injured people as an occupational therapist. Thanks, G.A.!

7. Elizabeth was the one I feared would be killed by her older brothers. I caught one of them stuffing her into the dryer when she was two, and at five she followed them in a leaping exercise off the roof of the dog house, missed the mark and broke her arm in three places. She helped me care for all of the above, the wounds have healed, and today she heals others' wounds as a loving, caring psychotherapist. Thanks, G.A.!

8. Tim put so much energy into being a guitar-strumming, long-haired hippie that we feared he would never be "normal." Ha! His high school teachers should see him now, the suave executive, whose "threads" have been replaced with a business suit, and his guitar with a briefcase. Thanks, G.A.!

9. Tom-the-terror, who knew no fears, who snatched bananas from gorillas at the zoo, played cops and robbers 'till we were sick with worry that he would be in prison before he was 21, is not a robber, but a cop who was honored for bravery when he snatched a gun from a suicide-attempt. Whew! Thanks, G.A.! (And hang in there. This one is still at risk.)

10. Rob-the-Righteous grew up bearing the burden of role model for the younger ones. With his investigative mind, he was continually taking apart appliances, seeking answers to the mysteries of the universe, and building rafts to float down the river. As a journalist he capitalized on that curiosity, and after winning awards for investigative reporting, he landed at the *New York Times*. Thanks, G.A.!

So those are my *"Ten Proofs for the Existence of Guardian Angels."* They may not impress theologians, but they sure have made a believer out of me.

AND TO THE VICTOR...

Watching Clinton and Bush go at one another so viciously in the presidential campaign of '92 made me nervous. I didn't understand why I reacted in such an emotional manner to a presidential election. But when I noticed Perot heckling on the sidelines, I remembered. A nagging memory rose to the surface, a fight between my three oldest boys when they were just barely more than toddlers.

Robbie was four, Tommie was three, and Timmie just 18 months old when I went to the hospital to give birth to our first daughter, Mary Beth. We were fortunate enough to find Nora, a wonderfully warm and wise farm woman to come in and take care of our three boys. Nora had a dimpled smile and the wisdom that comes with being a God-fearing Christian who had raised her own big brood while working the farm with her husband. To a woman who was accustomed to baking six loaves of bread and hanging several baskets of clothes on the line before the men came in for their breakfast of sausage, eggs, and fresh coffee cake, managing our household didn't seem too tough.

It wasn't long before Nora noticed that our eldest, Robbie, was being bullied by his younger brother, Tommie. Rather than hurt his little brother, whom he was taught to protect, Robbie would let Tommie snatch toys from him. Nora decided to teach Robbie to defend himself from these unfair attacks and fight for his rights.

One day the boys had finished their lunch and Nora explained that while she was baking pies for supper, she had only leftover desserts for lunch. She had one cookie, one piece of cake and one dish of chocolate pudding. Timmy, enthroned in the high chair, was offered the cookie, but the others were given a choice: pudding or cake.

As luck would have it, they both wanted the pudding. Robbie put in the first bid, so Nora gave him the pudding. Tommie promptly snatched the pudding from his older brother, who set up a howl. Realizing that he'd have to fight for it, Robbie reluctantly struck the first blow and soon the two of them were down on the floor, fists and feet flying. Nora watched them go at it, letting them pummel one another until one of them was lying kicking and screaming with a nose bleed, and the other finally stumbled to his feet, the victor. Bruised and battered, but a victor no less, ready to claim the spoils: the chocolate pudding.

But where was the prize? The pudding was not on the table where they had left it. Nor was the cake. Both boys looked to Nora in bewilderment. And the wise Nora simply smiled her dimpled smile and silently pointed to the high chair within easy reach of the table, where little Timmy sat happily shoving the last chunk of cake into a mouth circled with chocolate pudding. Then he grinned a smug grin of enormous satisfaction, while his battle-scarred brothers stared in dumb amazement.

Did Timmy need three desserts? No. Did he deserve three desserts? Absolutely not! It was simply a matter of snatching the victory from the two who had become so absorbed in defending themselves that they lost sight of the prize.

You see why I was nervous seeing Bush and Clinton fight for their lives while Ross Perot sat smugly on the sidelines?

BESTEST DRIVER IN THE WHOLE WORLD

E very time I see my children carefully lift and strap our grandchildren into one of those modern miracles of engineering, the car seat, I suffer pangs of guilt. Even though guilt is considered a trademark of the Catholic, I've never learned to live with it gracefully. So maybe by making a public confession of my crime I might alleviate some of the guilt before I do something foolish, like swap my silk camisole for a hair shirt.

Granted that people of my generation had never heard of a car seat, most of them exercised a little common sense when they learned to drive. Not me!

It took so long before Bob was out of school and working as a teacher that we already had three little ones and number four on the way before we dared to borrow the money for a car, and by then the situation was critical. We lived at the top of a hill in a small town in Minnesota, with no bus service and no mail delivery. In those days, grocery stores were not open evenings or Sundays, so my only means of shopping was dragging my three small boys downtown in our trusty, rusty little red wagon. That was easy, but bringing them and the groceries back was another thing. It was uphill all the way!

The year was 1952 and the car was a '41 Chevy Club Coupe, but it looked like a Rolls Royce to us. Our friends, Tom and Betty, drove us to St. Cloud to make the purchase, and Betty drove our new car back with me, giggling all the way. Bob had driven a few times in the Army, but this car handled a little different than a jeep, so he had to learn not to run up over curbs and bikes and things. I had never driven, but nothing would stop me from learning now!

Tom gave Bob a few lessons, and Betty was supposed to teach me, but she chickened out after the first two. Tom approached Bob at school and said, "I'm sorry, Bob, but I just can't let Betty teach Audrey to drive anymore. She's having nightmares, and I'm not feeling too hot myself 'cause she wakes me with her screaming."

I couldn't understand it. My kids told me in all sincerity, "Mommy, you are the bestest driver in the whole world." What did that dumb Betty know!

So the next day, when I needed more flour for the bread I was making, I did the reasonable thing. I asked myself, "Should I, in my pregnant condition, pull the kids and the flour in that little red coaster wagon?" The obvious answer was, "Heavens no!" After Bob left for school walking (the two blocks), I asked my kids, "Boys, who is the bestest driver in the whole world?"

"You are!" came the cheering chorus.

And so off we went! I had learned where all the important pedals were, but I hadn't quite mastered the clutch thing, but what the heck! I had learned how to run a temperamental old vacuum cleaner. Machines didn't scare me. The jerky stops and starts had all of us lurching, though, so I kept little one-year-old Timmy on the front seat beside me so I could put my arm out to prevent him from flying through the windshield. (I did that for so many years that now when I must come to a quick stop, I find myself still flinging my arm over anyone in the passenger seat regardless of age or seat belts.)

It wasn't long before things began to go wrong with the car. It had a funny habit of digging in its heels every so often and refusing to go in any direction but reverse. It did that once downtown in front of the post office and I had to travel the four blocks home in reverse, which can be tricky on Main Street. But I had Robby and Tommy posted in the back window to let me know if I was running off the road or into something.

I would have managed a whole lot better if people had minded their own business, but some smart aleck who ran a bar downtown told my husband, "Man, when I see that wife of yours coming down the street I give her the same right-of-way I would a police car or ambulance. I pull over to the side of the road. Way over!"

One day when I parked diagonally on Main Street, I happened to scrape a guy's bumper. Barely. No big deal, so I drove off. That night the owner came storming up to our house, pounded on the door, and demanded that my husband make it good. Bob got mad at me for not reporting it, but I explained my reason: it was only a bumper, and isn't that what bumpers are for? Bumping? How was I to know that a moment after I pulled away the dumb thing dropped off?

Years later, when those same three boys took driver's ed, they became very smug about their newly acquired driving skills, and soon they began hounding me to change my ways. "Stay in your lane!" they'd say, and when they saw me smile and wave at the passing car, "Mother, he wasn't waving at you! He was giving you the finger!"

Hmpf! So much for "the bestest driver in the whole world!"

HAIR WE ARE, LIKE IT OR NOT

I t's popular nowadays to point a finger at your parents and blame them for your problems. Well, I am an Adult Survivor of a Hair Nut. There now. I confessed and feel better already.

When I find myself going into convulsions over these shaved heads or the "bowl" haircuts I'm seeing, I know that there's no escaping my past.

Yes, my mother was a Hair Nut. Before I was born Mother was a hairdresser of sorts, working with one of those curling irons heated over a kitchen stove until it curled or singed the victim. When Mother looked at someone, she didn't see a person. She saw hair. This caused her to leap into marriage with the first beautiful head of curls that came along. When I was born, child number four, she looked at my full head of hair and escalated like an alcoholic turned loose in a brewery. She abandoned her career to devote full time to me. My head, that is.

For the first 12 years of my life, I was the victim of hair abuse. When other children could frolic outdoors, I was forced to sit upon a kitchen stool while my mother sectioned my hair into 6 to 10 thick roads running from the top of my head to my shoulder blades, painstakingly wet-brushed each section over her long fingers, wound them round and round until every end was secured, then carefully nudged them off her finger with a comb. Now could I run out to play? No, I had to sit there without moving until every hair was dry. (How do you think I got through the entire *Oz, Bobbsey Twins,* and *Nancy Drew* series? Thick hair takes time to dry.)

Still I wasn't safe. I never knew at what corner I might find the Hair Nut lurking, gleam in eye, brush in hand, waiting to snatch me and use me for her pleasure again. Some men stuff and mount their trophies. My mother clipped and boxed my curls, delivering them intact to my astonished family 45 years later. "Wow!" said the kids "It's Clairol 125, same as she uses now!"

Mother had a worse habit. She judged everyone by their hair. Her four daughters couldn't leave home without their crowning glory glowing and perfectly coiffed. Our only brother was dispatched to the barber with stunning regularity, Depression or no Depression. "If there's anything I can't stand," said Mother, "it's seeing these poor kids with their homemade haircuts. Put a bowl on their head and shave everything underneath!" (You see where I get it?)

This judging of others didn't get to me until the day she met my future husband. One Sunday morning Mother woke me to go to an early Mass. I told her, "No, today we must go to the last Mass. There you will meet the man I am going to marry. I met him last night, and Mother, he's perfect!" (Bob had no idea, of course, that his fate was being written in stone. He merely puzzled over why this crazy girl wanted to know what Mass he went to.) We arrived at Church ten minutes early, and I was frantic by the time he arrived, ten minutes late. "There he is!" I whispered to Mother as the usher led this slim, handsome hunk to the front pew. "Well, what do you think?" I grinned.

Mother sniffed, "He needs a haircut."

All the years we raised our ten children I prided myself on being less "harried about hair" while keeping their heads respectable. We obviously couldn't afford to take our five boys to the barber as often as they needed it, so I convinced Bob to learn the art of haircutting without getting "the bowl" look. It was trial and error all the way, and it left its mark on the poor kids. Bob was, at best, a reluctant barber, but I nagged him into keeping the boys in shape. When someone once commented on the boys "fresh haircuts," I wondered how they guessed fresh. "It's the blood," said Bob wryly.

New scientific evidence sheds light on HNA (Hair Nut Anxiety) Recently our eldest son gave a New Jersey barber his usual instructions: No clippers. "Why not?" the barber asked. "Because my hair is like wire. It breaks clippers. My dad broke more clippers on me!"

"Oh, yeah? Well, tell me. Did he ever get so mad he threw the clippers down?"

Rob nodded. "Sure, all the time."

"That's what broke the clippers!" said the wise barber.

Mother had her effect on our daughters, too. When Gretchen was little she'd say, "I hate it when Grandma says, `Gretchen, go get Grandma's purse.' I just know what's coming. She's going to get out her comb and fuss with my hair again." Today Gretchen is a hairdresser with her own salon, clearly demonstrating the far-reaching effects of this genetic strain.

Mother spent her declining years as a Recovering Hair Nut. We tried to educate her into noticing other things about people, such as their brilliance or wit, or the fact that they got along without arms or legs. The last time we visited her, she was on her death bed, and opened her eyes just enough to murmur a weak hello.

Bob had sneaked past my sister's dog waringly, to approach Mother's bedside. My niece Nancy said, "Oh, look, Uncle Bob, Nappy likes you now. He didn't growl at you this time." At this my mother opened both eyes and murmured, "That's because Nappy thinks he's a girl—his hair is so long."

Once a Hair Nut always a Hair Nut. Why fight it?

JESUS WEARS HIS SEATBELT
AND OTHER
AMAZING DEDUCTIONS

When our son, Tim, phoned to tell us Dylan's story, it reminded me of other similar tales that point up this theory. Dylan is our five-year-old grandson, whose flair for drama is matched only by his father's. One night they were driving to their home in Littleton, Colorado, when Dylan noticed the cross glowing high up on the side of the mountain. He wanted to know what it was doing there.

"Well, " said Tim, "I suppose it's to make us think about Jesus."

"Oh, I think about him all the time!" exclaimed Dylan. "Do you know He is everywhere, Dad? In fact He's right here—in the back seat."

"Really?" said Tim, impressed by the power of his son's convictions.

"Yep! And ya know what? He's got his seatbelt on!"

Dylan made a logical deduction. Good boys always fasten their seatbelts. Jesus is a good boy. Therefore, Jesus wears his seatbelt. It's a syllogism of pure logic that anyone should have been able to figure out, but it takes a five-year-old to put it together.

This story took me back more than 35 years when his father was about three. We had bought *The Little Book About God*, with charming illustrations by Ade Bethune. It began with the Creation and went on to Adam and Eve and the doctrine of original sin. Our three oldest boys loved it so much that they demanded to hear it over and over until they had it memorized. One day when a friend was visiting us, Timmy brought out the book and read it to her. He launched into such a dramatic rendition of Adam and Eve that everyone was spellbound.

"And so God said, 'Adam and Eve, you get outa this garden and don't you ever come back! He was real mad!"

"Goodness!" said our friend, "What had they done ?"

Timmy pounded on the book, exclaiming, "Can't you see? Can't you see? They were running around in their bare butts!"

Another logical deduction. It's naughty to run around without your clothes on, so what more reason did God need to kick them out? Forget the apple !

Nothing makes us more aware of the powerful influence we have on our children than to be smacked with this kind of logic, seeing them take two and two and come up with something other than four, but just as logical. It demonstrates how we provide the yardstick by which they measure the world around them. From the moment they start school, however, we realize somewhat painfully that we relinquish the role of Primary Authority to their primary teacher.

Our first three were boys—rascals with records before they ever got to school—setting the garage on fire, building a raft to float down the river, and stuffing their little sister into the clothes dryer. We couldn't wait to send them to a parochial school where they could "get religion." Like most parents, however, we soon learned that parochial schools don't work with the sudden impact of a Billy Graham conversion. You can put these little rascals into the cassocks of a Mass server, and be moved to tears at their appearance of holy innocence. That just serves to throw you off guard, though.

When Mary Beth was ready for first grade, we sent her to a nearby public school because she was nursing a broken arm. We had no idea how concerned she was about being deprived of the parochial education of her brothers, until one day she announced that they had learned a new prayer, "But don't worry, I changed the words." It was a prayer to the flag, she said, but when everyone else says, "And to the republic for which it stands," our daughter, hand on heart, eyes cast heavenward, would recite, "And to the recatholic for which it stands."

So the next year, when the arm was healed, Mary Beth joined her brothers in the parochial school, and soaked in the religion like cornflakes in milk. Before a year passed she vowed that she would be a nun, like the wonderful role models she had before her each day, a vow she would repeat regularly for the next three years.

Imagine my surprise, then, with her sudden change of heart when she was about 11. To prepare her for menstruation, I had been telling Mary Beth the story of the little egg that comes down into the uterus each month, and what happens if it is not fertilized, and how it becomes a baby if it is fertilized. I avoided unnecessary details by emphasizing the wonder of it all.

"Just think!" I said, "Every little girl is born with thousands of tiny eggs in her body that could turn into babies!"

"Oh, my gosh!" she exclaimed. "And to think I was going to be a nun!"

"Well, why not?" I asked.

"Are you kidding? And waste all those eggs?"

Once again, a child made a logical deduction. You shouldn't waste what God gives you, so don't waste your eggs.

So now we've lost our kids as income tax deductions. From the save quarters of the rocking chair, it's good to remember the other kinds of deductions our kids made. These scenes on the replay mode are a lot like the grandchildren: lots of fun and none of the responsibility.

Hmmm. Don't waste eggs. . .Don't run around in your bare butt. . .Jesus wears His seatbelt. Kids make the most amazing deductions, don't they?

LOVE AFFAIR WITH READING

About the time that I was expecting our tenth (and last!) child, a neighbor asked me how two people who obviously valued education could bring so many children into the world.

"How do you think you can provide for their education?" she asked. "Don't you want them to go to college?"

The answer was that yes, of course, we wanted each and every one of them to achieve their full potential, and yes, of course, that was our responsibility, but that did not necessarily mean a fat bank account. Our responsibility was to provide them with a love of learning. They could take it from there.

A love affair with reading is basic to a love of learning. Our children were brought up in a world of books. They learned to bring home library books and school books at their own risk. With parents who were teaching, selling textbooks (or sometimes encyclopedias) and usually enrolled in courses themselves, the books around the house outweighed the dirty laundry and dirty dishes combined. They had better keep track of their own books or earn the wrath of teachers and librarians.

Dad's authority stemmed from Scripture, Shakespeare, and Scientific Evidence, all of which he quoted with equal gusto. The kids soon learned to prove their points with similar tactics, frequently springing from the dinner table and returning moments later brandishing the weapon of choice with which to defeat their opponent: a book!

"Listen to this!" they'd exclaim, and then launch into a dramatic reading from their "authority."

Characters from books became family friends as we discussed them or made references to them. Thus even before learning to read, a child spoke of them as if they lived down the street. Robbie was only five when a visitor asked about an elaborate drawing he had made of three witches stirring a big pot over a fire. "Why, those are the three witches from Macbeth," he informed her. (His father was teaching Macbeth at the time.)

Once when four-year-old Gretchen wanted to get into a discussion among her older siblings about Lincoln, someone tried to shush her with, "You don't even know who Lincoln was!"

Gretchen was indignant. "Oh, yes, I do!" she protested. "Winken, Lincoln, and Nod!"

Reading turned out to be the one hobby we could always afford. It required no capital outlay for uniforms, equipment, or dues. In a public library or in a public school everyone was equal. Money didn't talk, but words did. Between the covers of books we found entertainment, knowledge, and inspiration.

Because we loved language and had little money to spend on frills, we played a great many word games with our children. We had Scrabble and Boggle, of course, but we also made up games with the dictionary to play in the car on long trips, or huddled in the basement during a storm. Some we still play today when our children and grandchildren are visiting.

Reading aloud "with expression" became a favorite pastime. Since we loved to ham it up ourselves, the children could hardly wait to learn to read fluently so that they, too, could dramatize a story for their younger siblings.

Our children learned that with reading they could do anything, learn anything, be anything. Want to make a birdhouse? Get a book! Want to learn about General Atkinson and the Black Hawk war? Get a book! Want to be a teacher, lawyer, doctor or scuba-diver? With the right books. . .

Most of our children have college degrees, even advanced degrees, but not because we saved for their education. They put themselves through school and some are still at it. One in her thirties is a college freshman, but undaunted by years and the responsibilities of running a beauty shop and rearing two children. She learned early in life that education is a lifelong process. She remembers attending her mother's college graduation along with the other nine siblings.

Maybe it's wishful thinking, but I like to believe that our children value their education more because they didn't have a free ride. Motivation was never a problem once they developed a love affair with reading and a corresponding thirst for knowledge.

Whether or not they ever go to college, is not nearly as important, however, as their learning how to learn. The quality of my life could never be what it is today had I not read about how to teach kids composition and grammar, how to take care of my health, prepare microwave meals, use a computer and modem, write a novel, and all of the other peculiar interests I have. It's that kind of reading that can make anyone richer and happier.

Parents can offer their high school graduates the fattest bank account which they have sacrificed to build, but if they haven't first given them a true love of reading, it won't buy a college degree. And what's worse, they will be deprived of their primary source of nourishment for life.

What must parents teach their kids? To love God, love one another, and love reading.

Gospel according to Fixmers!

Okay, can anyone think of a better legacy?

TAX TIME IS HAPPY TIME

These days there is very little I do for my daughter Patty, but each year I have the privilege of doing her income taxes. To see Patty and her husband Ernie join the ranks of Americans who support, rather than drain their country, gives me great satisfaction. The higher her taxes, the happier I am.

Patty was born thirty-three years ago—retarded. She was our eighth child and just as beautiful with her dimpled smile and curly hair as the others. We sensed a problem, however, when she was about three months old. She didn't reach for bright objects. Was she blind? She didn't respond to sounds. Could she be deaf? But at feeding time she quickly turned to the sound of the spoon stirring her cereal, and she opened her mouth when the spoon approached. She was neither deaf nor blind.

After a call to the public library, requesting "All the best books on mental retardation," I embraced each author with a frantic plea for clues. "An easy baby to care for, sleeps a great deal, appears at times to be deaf or blind. . ." My heart sank. They were describing my baby. It was not until I got to the book by a pioneer in special education, Sister Theodore, O.S.F., of nearby St. Coletta School, however, that I found a spark of hope. She wrote glowingly about these special children who were the most loved by God and the most loving.

Nevertheless, we prayed, cried, and worried our way through the next few months, because deep in our hearts we knew. When we finally took Patty to Madison for three days of diagnostic tests, we sat stiff and tense across the desk from a tall, distinguished doctor.

He was brisk and to the point. "Your daughter is mentally retarded, and when this is apparent at such a young age, you can be sure it is serious."

I wanted to protest that maybe we just looked harder than most people. But who was I to argue with such a smart doctor? I was brought up to believe the doctor knows everything!

So Bob and I sat silently listening to "the team's interpretation" of each test, and held our breaths. "We recommend you put her in an institution now. It wouldn't be fair to the other children to bring her home. because she will demand a lot of attention," he said confidently. When he saw the look of horror on our faces, he added, "Of course, you could take her home if you insist. Some folks think they make nice pets."

That did it! Bob jumped to his feet, shouting, "If that's all you have to say, we'll leave. . .with our daughter."

Today doctors are better trained to work with parents who are hurting, and the diagnostic tools are improved. At that time, however, only the Holy Spirit could have guided us to follow our instincts. With an "I'll show them!" attitude, Bob turned his anger into a powerful force behind a program of exercises he himself devised. That first summer he worked with Patty on a blanket at the beach, teaching her to sit up and then to creep, while I supervised the other children in the water. Bob was sure of himself, but I took longer to overcome my attitude that doctors knew it all.

Teaching Patty, watching her develop, became the focal point of our family life. Everyone had a part in it. She was only eighteen months old when she took her first steps, and we all gathered around in a big circle on the living room floor. In a pink ruffled dress with layers of can-cans poking out beneath, Patty looked like a little princess. She had taken only a few steps when such a loud cheer erupted from her brothers and sisters that she dropped to her seat, clapped her hands and joined in the applause.

When we enrolled Patty as a preschool day-student at St. Coletta, she learned that she was worthwhile. I remember when she was six, watching her stand before the mirror, trying to coordinate the brush strokes with her reverse image. In frustration she threw down the brush and exclaimed, "Oh, Patty, you are too tupid!" The pang of sorrow I felt quickly changed to joy, however, when she added, "But that's all right. That's the way God made you."

Patty attended public school in special education classes for the next 12 years. Our emotions through those years ran the full gamut: thrills when she learned to read and write, pain when we saw how desperately she tried to do everything her sisters did. Pretty as she might be, no boy would ever ask her to the prom.

After high school, we sent her back to St. Coletta School for their work training program. It was the best money we ever spent. There she learned the dignity of menial work of all kinds, and the meaning of responsibility. That experience, combined with her father's training in saving money, produced a young woman who entered the workforce with the determination of an Amazon slaying dragons.

In just a few months, the St. Coletta Work Program had placed Patty at the Fireside Restaurant and Playhouse, where she has worked as a dishwasher for more than ten years. In the Fireside kitchen, Patty met and fell in love with another dishwasher from St. Coletta, and four years ago they were married in a touching ceremony in the lovely chapel of their alma mater. They keep their apartment clean, budget their money, and pay taxes.

In the eyes of the world, our other children may be more successful, but it is Patty who makes us most proud. You'll forgive me if I boast a little when I do her taxes.

Growing Old Gracefully

GROWING OLD GRACEFULLY

When I was married only four years, I brought out our framed wedding picture and hung it on the wall. A few minutes later I heard my three-year-old say to his little brother, "Tommy, come and see the picture of Daddy and the pretty lady." I knew in that instant that growing old gracefully would not be easy.

One dictionary defines grace as "a beauty of form, movement, or manner; pleasing or agreeable quality." The image that springs to mind is that of a lovely ballerina flitting through the air. But the reality of old age is sore feet, a stony spine, and arthritic joints. So growing old gracefully has got to be the ultimate challenge of life.

Beauty of form and movement? Like getting in and out of cars? So let's say you've been cramped into the passenger side for two or three hours, and you know that someone you haven't seen in years is watching for your arrival, ready to do a quick assessment of your aging process. The thing to do is exercise your upper body along the way by twisting around every few minutes for a kernel of popcorn from the back seat. In other words, the kind of movements that kept you limber when the kids were small, breaking up fights and wiping noses. Then pull over a mile or two before the arrival point (preferably a secluded spot), slowly pry yourself loose from the car, and do ten minutes of vigorous hip twists, leg kicks, and knee bends. That way, we won't scandalize anyone with slow, stumbling movements and creaking bones on arrival. We will emerge with that "beauty of form and movement" of the TV models demonstrating cars. (Sure!)

As for manner, I guess that includes attitude. We must try to give the impression that we have no more concern for safety than the average forty-year-old. With heads held high, we look sure-footed and confident. Recently I had the opportunity to observe elderly people walking briskly along the beach in Puerto Rico. I wondered what it was besides their healthy tans that gave them such a youthful appearance. Then it dawned on me—they didn't have to watch out for icy patches like the shuffling seniors in Wisconsin. Four or five months of studying where to place our feet is enough to cripple us so we can't straighten up to see the first robin in Spring.

"A pleasing or agreeable quality." When the mirror shouts, "Danger! Falling flab and deep wrinkles!" but the spouse says, "Honey, you're beautiful!" we must not hit him with a frying pan for lying, but should smile graciously, remembering that the poor dear's eyesight is failing at a corresponding rate. It's God's way of rewarding us for sticking together so long.

It's a bad idea to call attention to the clock running. I remember my great Aunt Lizzy for two things: the yummy Black Cows she always served, using her homemade root beer and rich ice cream, and her gloomy reminders that "This might be my last Christmas (or Fourth of July or whatever)." I recently figured out that she began saying this in her early fifties, and she lived to be eighty! We would have quit visiting Aunt Lizzy much earlier, I fear, if it were not for her wonderful Black Cows.

It's important for all of us to be in touch with our mortality. When the good teaching nuns told us to be ready for death by being in the state of grace, we knew they were referring to another kind of grace entirely. It was the kind of beauty and ease of movement that would allow us to glide into heaven when we were called, a kind of boarding pass, if you will. Still, as kids, we just thought dying was a strange and fearful thing, that a corpse was spooky, and that people who talked about death were morbid.

In the natural course of events we are initiated to the reality of death gradually. As kids we see animals and grandparents die. As we grow older we attend more and more funerals of our peers, and we do a mortality check by averaging out the ages in the obituary column. The older we get, the less fearsome is death.

I had forgotten how differently we see death at 60 than we did at 35 until a recent occurrence. We had attended the funeral of a friend who died after a lingering illness, which made the finality more bearable. I found several elements of that funeral so appealing that I began to think, "Now, that's the way I'd like to have mine." I was moved to see each of his grandchildren placing a rose on his casket, symbolizing his own life going on in his progeny. The interment would take place in his home town, so following the funeral Mass there was a happy gathering of old friends for dinner before the funeral procession would begin the 70 mile trip. Great idea!

It had bothered us to think about being buried in the town in which we raised our children, since none of them would be living there in the future. A hometown burial sounded right. We would be with our parents, brothers and sisters and generations of cousins and aunts and uncles. So we happily made the arrangements and felt a great weight lifted off our shoulders. We told our daughter about the lovely site we had selected, a true church yard where people frequently gathered for stations of the cross, and we had a spot next to my parents and right by the fourth station. Perfect! And what did my daughter say? "Oh, no! That's so morbid!" And then she promptly called all her brothers and sisters to warn them that Mom and Dad had really lost it now.

So this challenge of growing old gracefully is a big one, indeed. It means keeping limber, smiling through pain, flying South in the winter when you can, and finally preparing for death without boring kinfolk with the details. . .unless you can offer them homemade Black Cows.

KEEPING AN EYE
ON THE OBITUARIES

Mark Twain once said that he always checked the obituaries to be sure he wasn't listed. That's stretching it a bit, but as with everything Twain wrote, there was a bit of truth in it. The truth is that the older we get, the quicker we turn to the obituary column.

It's not just that we know more candidates either, because even when we don't recognize a single name, we check out one thing: their ages. After a bit of mental arithmetic, we come up with the average for the day, just to see how we're doing. It's what I call, "taking my longevity temperature." My idea of a good day is when the Dow Jones and the Obituary Average are in the high nineties. It makes me feel like planting a tree, starting a Ph.D. program, or even a James Michener novel.

When I find myself playing these average games with the obituary column, I am haunted by the jokes I used to make about my grandmother's and even my mother's obsession with death.

"The only thing on Grandma's social calendar these days are funerals!" I'd quip. "They'll never come to yours, Grandma."

Or I'd wisecrack, "Just give Mother the obituary page and she'll be happy."

"You just wait until you get to be my age!" Mother would answer in her somber tones.

Well, I'm getting there now, Mother, and I'm still interested in many things besides obituaries, but I must confess that I do check them, just in case.

Back when I was a kid, Grandmas wore simple house dresses and starched bib aprons around the house. When they went to funerals they were properly attired in black. It's like they began rehearsing for their own funerals from the time they hit 40.

The Church taught us to "be prepared for death." In Grandma's youth, however, receiving Holy Communion was restricted to special occasions, and then only immediately following Confession. Consequently being prepared for death meant praying a great deal and hoping a priest could come galloping in on his great white charger, armed with holy oils and Eucharist, to say the magic words that would send their soul straight to heaven.

It was no coincidence that the sacrament of the dying was called Extreme Unction. It was extreme, all right. And after putting a priest to all that trouble, you darn well better die! A few false alarms and you might find yourself in the predicament of the boy who cried wolf.

Grandma had the same kind of reverence for doctors as she did for priests. If the doctor put her on a diet, she would follow it religiously. If a pastor suggested a rosary every day, she said it. If he initiated a novena, she made it!

As I look back on it now, it seems rather sad that our ancestors had to rely so heavily on taking directions from those in authority, instead of learning the facts and taking responsibility for making decisions themselves. But knowledge was not so readily available in those days. And doctors often hid the diagnosis from a patient, lest they upset them. And even when they did disclose a diagnosis like "cancer," it was barely whispered, and the patients kept the secret buried, even from their own families! This surely compounded their suffering immeasurably.

Along with a looser dress code and support groups that encourage open dialogue, today's grannies enjoy more security with God, too. I remember Grandma praying for a happy death. What she had in mind was lying propped up in bed, with a rosary twined about her fingers, her family gathered about, weeping and praying, and a priest anointing her as he intoned his prayers in Latin. And she hoped it wouldn't happen before age 65.

Thanks to the Church's new emphasis on living in the state of grace and frequent participation in the Eucharist, I've revised my thinking. Now my idea of a happy death is to drop over in the middle of an aerobics class following daily Mass and communion. . .at age 102!

I can just hear my husband muttering, "I told that crazy woman all that exercise would kill her!"

IN PRAISE OF THE CLUBHOUSE

Sometimes we grandparents get the feeling that we might be out of touch. The kids today who cut their teeth on microchips and slay Nintendo dragons appear to have little in common with us oldies who clamped roller skates over shoes with a key and proved our dexterity by winning more marbles or jacks. But just when we begin to get the message, "Time to check out?" the grandchild pulls us briefly into his world and we find it thoroughly familiar. I know this world, we think, because I've been there.

Such was the case on a summer day several years ago when our grandson, Andy, was seven years old. We were visiting their country home when Andy took us by the hand and led us to his clubhouse. Beyond the gravel drive we trudged, past the scarlet peonies nodding their friendly greeting. Machinery and livestock had long since vanished, for it was no farmer, but an editor and his family with a love of country living that now held the mortgage on this land. We plodded on down a path cut through the tall grass by the steady pounding of little feet.

Finally we halted before a strange assembly of boards nailed at right angles to a tree branch. "This," declared Andy proudly, "is our clubhouse!"

I looked at the sturdy old oak tree, itself like some permissive grandparent, cheerfully accommodating a youngster by bending to his level. Dozens of nails had been driven helter-skelter by some happy hammer into the sturdy arm of the old oak. Finally one or two had hit and held, and behold! Andy had his side wall and with it his shelter from the world.

As Grandpa praised Andy for his carpentry skills, I was caught up in a web-like mist of memories, memories of my childhood in the 1930s and The Clubhouses I have known.

Schuler's tool shed . Had it once housed a horse? Maybe so, but that place cleaned up real nice after we stacked up the old issues of *Liberty* and *Saturday Evening Post,* swept up the rusty nails, and pulled the old leather harnesses off the walls.

Nary a thought did we have of valuable antiques, of course, just "old stuff!"

Roesch's old meat market! That store stood abandoned throughout the Depression, but provided us with a theatre. The store windows upfront became two stages where we could perform our dances after rehearsing them in the back room between the old counters and stored furniture.

Still deep in thought as we drove home from our son's house, I asked my husband, "What purpose do you think a clubhouse fills in a kid's life?"

"It's where little boys find out about girls!" he answered with a wicked grin.

Bob was right, I thought, remembering tales of forbidden magazines and pin-up calendars. But it was so much more!

In your clubhouse you could escape from the problems of the adult world—Mother crying because Daddy lost his job, the radio blasting Father Coughlin's angry attacks on the New Deal or the Recovery Act—frightening sounds to a little girl.

And for good or ill, a clubhouse meant we could be exclusive. There we could try out our developing notions of status and unity. Restricted membership! The Miller kids couldn't join because they swore and smelled bad. We'd heard rumors that Henry, the twelve-year-old, rolled his own cigarettes with Bull Durham. Marilyn Jones could join, despite the fact that she was a tattle-tale and a brat, because her indulgent mother would provide us with an old table as well as cookies and Kool-Aid.

A clubhouse was a hide-out. It was a place you could duck into when it was time to do dishes or clean your room. When you just had to read a few more chapters to find out how Nancy Drew captured the jewel thief, you needed such a haven.

A clubhouse was a refuge of freedom from authority. You could arrange the orange-crate furniture any way you liked. You could eat crackers and drink Kool-Aid without worrying about crumbs messing up the floor and sugar drawing ants.

A clubhouse was a fortress against the enemy—when the Miller kids attacked with their sling-shots, when Daddy took off his belt, when Mama discovered the broken window—these were times when a kid needed a fortress.

What happened to all those clubhouses? What made our tightly-knit circles unravel? It seemed that in each case the truth gradually dawned on us. You had to have rules. A leader emerged, the kid with the most fertile imagination or the loudest voice or the biggest allowance. We voted, of course, on important issues like how much dues to charge, or how much admission for the sensational shows we put on. But day-to-day issues, such as who had the right to talk, was decided by The Leader. As the list of rules grew longer someone had to record them and someone else enforced them.

When the accumulated property began to fill up the clubhouse, it became apparent that somebody had to clean the place. Since Jane was the leader, and Judy directed the play, it was only fair that Marilyn did the cleaning. This didn't set well with Marilyn, because the furniture and free lunches were supplied by her mother. War is declared.

It's the beginning of the end. What had begun as an escape from the world of rules and regulations and no respect has now reverted to a mini society that looks suspiciously like the first. Too darn much like the Real World! So little by little, we abandon the Clubhouse, carrying with us a deeper understanding of society.

The boundaries of our world expand. Our home becomes our fortress against a cruel world, the public library our hideaway, and we learn the meaning of "taking sanctuary in the church" when we face a crisis that calls for prayer, reflection, and faith.

In each of these societies we learn to accommodate, to compromise, to respect rules and authority. Why? Because we have been through the bootcamp. We are graduates of The Clubhouse.

So even though Andy and his generation have their Nintendos and their computers, they still need The Clubhouse as their training ground for the greater institutions of life: Family, Church, and State.

Three cheers for The Clubhouse !

THANKS for GIVING YEARS

One morning Bryant Gumbel on "Today" introduced his guest, a woman who had authored a book with this amazing premise: The safest sex is no sex and the best marriages are those in which the couple enters into the union as virgins. Save yourself for your spouse. I guess it's the latest thing!

Now isn't that the most remarkable discovery? It's right up there with those diet doctors a few years ago who discovered fasting once in awhile was good for the body. My first reaction to these "discoveries" is to groan audibly. My second is to whisper a prayer of thanksgiving for having been born into a generation who knew these things all along. We had a family and Church which taught them, and happy marriages which proved them.

Each time Thanksgiving rolls around we seniors have a little more to be thankful for. Oh, sure, we have a little more stiffness and pain in the joints, but the advantages of growing old far outweigh the disadvantages. And focusing on the pluses puts a smile on the face.

My good friend, Mary McBride, tells of a father who refused to allow his children more than five minutes a day to grouse about anything negative. He timed their complaints and forced them to switch to a pleasant subject when the time was up. Once when Mary asked if she skipped a day or two could she have additional time another day. He said, "Absolutely not! It's a privilege that's not cumulative."

The result was that the Duffy children were forced to look for the sunny side of every experience, the humor in every situation, no matter how frightening or gloomy. Mary credits this habit with a lifetime of laughter that has pulled her through the tough years of rearing her six children alone after the death of her husband. And since humor is so contagious, Mary McBride has caused an epidemic throughout the United States with her humorous books and her talks.

Her son, Father Bill McBride of St. William's Parish in Janesville, points out another of her traits that brings joy to all who know her. It was Phyllis Diller, for whom McBride wrote for many years, who told him, "Your mother is one of the most thankful people I have ever known."

Thankfulness is an attitude that brightens many days, yet all too often we hear of senior citizens who spend so much energy grousing about what they can no longer do that they forget to be thankful for all that they can do.

My mother had it, too. After my father died, Mother was always the concern of her neighbors. Knowing she lived alone, they watched to see if she raised her shades by 7 a.m. When she didn't they were right there with a visit or a phone call to check on her. I recall a grouchy older person who exclaimed, "Hmpf! How does she rate? If I was living alone no one would give a darn!" We all smiled knowingly. That was a "no-brainer," as our kids would say. She was a grouch and Mother was a smiling, happy senior who accepted help with grace and never failed to show her thankfulness for small favors.

I am thankful for such a mother and for the thankful friends with whom I am able to surround myself. One such example is a lifelong friend who lives in Minnesota. Her name is Patricia Gits Opatz, and she is well known in the St. Cloud

Diocese where she writes for St. John's Liturgical Press and, like McBride, gives many talks in dioceses throughout Minnesota and the Dakotas. Her fame has spread nationwide with her wise and sparkling meditations published as a series on the backs of church bulletins. Pat has the uncanny ability to write on spiritual subjects with a wit and sparkle one expects from an Erma Bombeck or a Mary McBride.

A good example is a phone call I received from Pat in early November. She was checking on plans for a proposed visit, but couldn't resist the temptation to sing for me. Sounds crazy? Well, that's the kind of relationship we have had since our college days at St. Ben's, forty-six years ago When one of us works on a speech or a program or writing that particularly excites us, we just have to bounce it off the other. Pat was preparing a talk for Catholic women in the St. Cloud Diocese. When I heard the song I begged her to send it to me so I could share it with the readers of my November column. It was a perfect fit. And here it is:

A SONG FOR OLDER WOMEN
ON DAYS WHEN THEY DON'T FEEL THANKFUL
by Patricia Gits Opatz
(to the tune of "My Bonnie Lies Over the Ocean")

I thank God I'm finally aging.
I welcome each line on my face.
I know that each new sag and wrinkle
brings dignity, wisdom and grace.

Chorus: So long, good-bye
to spring chicken days with their cares and strife.
Three cheers, golden years. . .
I've waited for this all my life!

I no longer weigh myself daily,
the larger dress sizes I choose.
I'm thankful my hair's turning silver
and love wearing sensible shoes.
        Chorus

Thank God I've survived all those tough years
of babies and bottles and bills.
I welcome the pleasures of aging:
retirement, trifocals and pills!
        Chorus

I thank God I'm not a teenager.
I found adolescence the pits.
With all of its weird clothes and hairdos,
its hormones, peer pressures and zits.
    Chorus

I thank God I married my husband
and not the guy who asked me first.
For even when we're having bad days,
I know that I could have done worse.
    Chorus

Yes, I am thankful for all of the above, too, and also for my happy mother and friends like McBride and Opatz.

There's one thing you ought to know about those two smiling friends. They are both women who have suffered bout after bout of cancer with all of its attending nightmares: the anxiety, the chemo, the nausea. Their delightful ability to inspire and make people laugh is the best health insurance I can think of. Ladies like that don't die alone.

BETTER TO GIVE
THAN TO RECEIVE:
(BETTER TO SHED THAN TO PILE ON)

W e senior citizens can remember, not too long ago, when the holiday season found us buried under an avalanche of glad tidings: making costumes for the boys' Christmas programs and whipping up dresses for the girls' delight, baking cookies for the classroom party, and replacing lost mittens or outgrown boots while nursing kids through chicken pox or flu. All of this meant relegating shopping to the last minute. But then again, that wasn't all bad. We found a lot of reduced prices at such times. Good thing, too, since by then we were swept along with so much Christmas spirit we could scarcely restrain our generosity.

Didn't we all dream of the day when we'd have more time to plan and shop for the right gift? And the money to buy what we wanted? And now that we are senior citizens that time is here, right?

Wrong! Now we have learned one of life's little ironies: As our wallets became stronger, our bodies weakened. Along with the new freedom of time came the restrictions of pain and stiffness in the joints. One quick jaunt around the smallest mall can send us hobbling to the next free bench available, ready to tackle anyone who tries to beat us to it.

When I first retired from teaching, I reveled in the luxury of being able to shop during school hours. I learned that the malls could be places of sanity after all. I gloried in the senior discounts for lunch, reveled in the Christmas music piped through the loud speakers, and trotted merrily along from one store to the next. This year, however, I can't bring myself to begin shopping, and once again I find myself brimming with admiration for those much smarter women who began in July and have every last gift wrapped already! Or they shop by catalogue and never miss a beat with back orders.

And some ambitious ladies make gifts all year. One friend of mine actually crocheted bedspreads for each of her ten children, doing one each year. Another artistic soul finds a pattern for some intriguing centerpiece or decorative item and then makes six identical masterpieces for each of her six sisters. And one grandmother knits a sweater for each granddaughter. It's just my luck that she is my granddaughters' "other grandma." It makes me feel downright incompetent.

But the best idea of all came from one of my daughters-in-law. "Why don't you do what my mother did?" she suggested. "Each year she gives the kids something she or Dad has kept for years. Last year she gave Emma a very old book she had when she was ten years old. It was a copy of *The Bobbsey Twins*. Emma cherishes it."

I immediately thought about things I had received from my mother when she sold her house back in the sixties. There were my copies of *The Bobbsey Twins* and *Nancy Drew Mysteries* and my favorite of all, Sigrid Undset's *Kristin Lavransdatter*. And then there were my old diaries, locks of my hair clipped when I was two years old, (But who would want those? My daughter, Gretchen, the hairdresser?) Elizabeth already asked for Bob's grandmother's china jewelry dish which had been an engagement present from Bob's grandfather in 1885. Now that's an heirloom! And we don't have to shop for it. Hmmm!

One of my friends recently had a son getting married, and she prepared a video to be played during the wedding reception. It was made up of snapshots of her son as he grew from babyhood to manhood, and pictures of his bride throughout her life, as well. She had cleverly set the whole thing to music and printed (on her computer) amusing subtitles for the various phases of their lives. The cost was surprisingly reasonable, and made a wonderful gift.

So why couldn't I do that? I must have thousands of snapshots, thanks to my sister, Grace, who had no children and plenty of film. Now, if I got started about January 1, I might have one video for each family member by next Christmas.

Yes, giving our children and grandchildren a sentimental gift, a part of their past, might be good for us as well. I have long felt the pressure to shed THINGS. We work all our lives to acquire THINGS and finally they become a burden to us. There's more to dust, more to move, more to step around, and more to take care of. No wonder scripture tells us it's harder for a rich man to get to heaven than for a camel to pass through the eye of a needle. He's loaded down with THINGS!

Christmas! Tis the season to be shedding! I'm dreaming of a Light Christmas . . .next year.

Retirement: Blues or Bliss?

etirement was a breeze for me. I guess that's because in all the twenty years I spent at home rearing my family and the twenty-three I spent teaching English, I had to fight down the urge to write about it instead of doing it. Five years before the 1990 self-imposed target, I renewed my study of the craft of writing and began free-lancing on the side. Armed with the tools of the trade (computer, printer, *Writer's Market*), the transition was smooth and joyful. And the twofold rewards of seeing my work in print and cashing the checks was the hot-fudge and nut topping on my frozen yogurt. Just desserts!

For my husband, it's another story. His work with a textbook publisher took him flying all over the country and speaking to teacher groups. He didn't have a hobby or a new career in mind when the "offer he couldn't refuse" came on

June 1. As much as I loved having him home every night, I couldn't help worrying that some of the scary tales I had heard about retired husbands "getting in the way" and "controlling" might apply in our case.

I began plotting ways to make it a smooth transition for Bob from "Speaker of the Workshop" to "Speaker of the House." For starters, I thought about finding a special tape to put on our tape player, so I could punch a button about every hour. A tape of applause, that is.

I knew he'd miss flying, so I figured I might serve his lunch on a tiny plastic tray, with yards of plastic wrap enclosing the mystery sandwich. And I could whip up some "frequent stay-at-home" plan which would reward him for each trip to the grocery store (10 points), Kentucky Fried Chicken (15). He could cash in his points for such varied awards as an annual membership to the local health club or a free round trip to the zoo with a grandchild of his choice. When he returned from the store, I could stand behind the counter in the kitchen and check his bags for him, then three out of ten times lose them.

I soon noticed that, despite my years of experience in writing out creative lesson plans, Bob was no better than my former students in carrying out his assignments. (I've had experience in dealing with that one, too!) Then I realized that

I could follow the example of his office. I'd dispatch his week's assignments every Saturday by overnight express. So far it hasn't been necessary, because he's still working on the first one: cleaning his office, garage, and basement of 30 years of accumulated books and brochures. He feels compelled to read each paper before tossing it.

Maybe it's because I did work outside my home and now enjoy burying myself in my office that I don't have a problem with a "territorial imperative." Now that women have broadened their work scope and men no longer feel threatened by helping with housework, it's easier to arrive at an equitable division of labor. Bob has already mastered the vacuum cleaner and is working hard on learning to load the dishwasher.

It turns out Bob's retirement is a happy arrangement for me. I no longer have to spend my Sundays doing laundry, nor my Friday nights racing the dog to the front door so that I could get the first kiss. And soon we won't have to include book bags as part of our living room furniture. It got so bad years ago already that I quit fighting it. At Christmas time, I'd simply drop a white cloth over the pile and stick a manger scene on top. Our kids grew up thinking Jesus was born on a mountain top.

One of the nicest rewards, though, is having my husband enjoy going to daily Mass with me. Our parish has many retired couples in attendance, but just enough widows and widowers to serve as a reminder that being a couple carries with it a time limit. Nevertheless, it's a feeling that although our own family is grown and our work family dissolved, we still belong to a family of worshippers. It gives us such a warm feeling each day as we leave church amid smiles and cheerful greetings.

"Isn't it wonderful, dear?" I asked my husband as we left Mass one day, "that so many retired people start their day like this?"

"Yes, but it shouldn't surprise you," answered my highly experienced educator. "We're all cramming for our finals!"

Now if I could just get this man, who never missed a flight in 30 years, to make it to church on time! I guess I'll have to install a public address system and announce, "Final boarding call. Last flight for St. Joseph's leaving at Gate One."

HARTWICK TELLS POLISH CHICKEN STORIES

"**H**ave you heard the one about the Polish chicken?"

When John Hartwick asks that question, everyone in the Communion Breakfast Club sets down his coffee cup and listens closely, because we know it's no joke, but another profound lesson about life that this doctor, now retired from medical practice, has learned from his new career as a poultry farmer.

After weekday Mass, a large group of Eucharistic Celebrators gather in one or another of Fort Atkinson's friendly restaurants, and celebrate retirement by relaxing over a leisurely cup of coffee and swapping stories or opinions or recipes. We've been following, with rapt attention, the amazing story of John Hartwick's Polish Chicken.

It began in Spring when Hartwick, glowing with pride, told us that his babies had been delivered. It was an assortment of 250 baby chicks including one Polish chicken.

"Okay, what's a Polish chicken?" we asked dutifully in the droll tone one might say, "Who's there?" to a boring knock-knock joke.

So the next day, Hartwick brought along his poultry catalog to show us there really was such a thing as a Polish Chicken, and that its appearance is unmistakable. We gasped in disbelief at the picture of this all black chicken with the most incredible white plumage for a crown. It was positively regal!

Three weeks later Hartwick told us the sad fate of the chicken. He found it lying in the manure-filled gutter, all of its lovely crown ripped out, half dead. It was clearly the victim of racial discrimination among the all white chickens. Dr. Hartwick's diagnosis? It had suffered a stroke after the attack and was paralyzed on one side. He had no choice but to segregate it into a little infirmary he had devised for the sick and the handicapped of the poultry society.

The Polish chicken had a roommate. In June a baby goose had been hatched in the Hartwick OB ward. (It's the least one could expect from an M.D.) Not wanting the tiny goose to be subjected to the taunts of the much older (teenage) geese, Hartwick had placed that baby in the infirmary. Now the Polish Chicken, limp and barely alive, was placed in the infirmary, too. When the good doctor made his rounds the next day, he was alarmed to see the goose, too, picking at the bloody head of the Polish chicken. On closer inspection, however, Hartwick discovered the amazing truth. The little goose was carrying water in its beak and releasing it, drop by drop, on the head of the Polish chicken. She was washing the poor head and preening the black feathers.

"Mother Goose!" I exclaimed.

"John the Baptizer," said Bob.

"We need a name for the Polish Chicken," someone commented.

Jim and Bunnie Tate are regulars at the Communion Breakfast Club, and Jim had a suggestion. "Name it Jim because it's just like me. I'm bald and had a stroke, too." Then he patted his wife's hand and added, "But I didn't need a goose to nurse me. I have a Bunnie."

We urged Hartwick to bring his Polish chicken and nurse goose to the parking lot of St. Joseph Church for the blessing of animals on the feast of St. Francis. Never have two animals created more excitement than these two. We all gathered around as Hartwick carefully lifted the chicken and then the goose from their crate. Watching the large hands of the doctor lovingly stroke the feathers of this now beautiful Polish chicken, and cradle the frightened goose beneath his arm, we understood St. Francis a little better.

WE'VE COME A
LONG WAY. . .MAYBE

Did modern woman evolve from a doormat? That's the question asked by cartoonist Marian Henley. She offers the answer in 8 pictures and 30 words.

In the first frame we see a flat glob on the floor saying, "Oh, it's all right! Go ahead and walk all over me!" In the next three frames the glob gradually takes the form of a woman rising, first head and shoulders, then torso, until she is finally on her feet but crouched in caveman posture, saying, "I really. . ." When she raises her head, "I really do mind." And in the final frame, she stands erect shouting, "So watch your step!"

I love that cartoon. To me it is a reminder that I was fortunate to have been born in the late 1920s because I have witnessed, first hand, this exciting evolution of woman. Watch? No, I'm not one to watch a parade marching by. I rather leaped on board to join in the celebration of women.

Already in second grade I knew what I was going to be when I grew up. I would be a writer. How did I know? "Sistersez!" It was Sister Bernadette, my second grade teacher, who read my story to the class, saying, "Audrey is going to be a writer." And at that age, anything that "Sistersez" is an adjunct to the Ten Commandments.

It wasn't until I was a senior at Madonna High School that I realized what a treacherous war was raging out there. I'm not referring to W.W. II now, even though the year was 1945. I'm thinking about the battle of the sexes. It took a comment from my grandfather to spell it out for me.

Maureen Daly came to Aurora that year. I'm talking about THE Maureen Daly, 21-year-old best-selling author of *Seventeenth Summer*. I was dazzled by Daly, and so I wangled permission from our principal to go hear her speak and to interview her for our school paper. Reporters from other school papers and the local press were there too, of course, but somehow I managed to capture her attention with one of my questions, and she continued to address me personally throughout most of the interview. I was ecstatic! I floated home in a cloud of rapture!

When I arrived, I burst through the front door and exploded my account of my thrilling experience. Mother stopped me in mid-rapture to point out that my grandparents were there and where were my manners? "Say hello, for goodness sake, and tell them who this woman is."

I obediently paid my respects to my grandparents and proceeded to run through the litany of Daly's achievements: the novel published at 21, the best-selling status, all the awards.

My German-born grandparents clung to the theory that girls should not go to high school, much less college. They waited stoically until I finished my dramatic rendition, and then Grandpa shook his head sadly, "Yeah, but I vunder, can she clean a chicken?" I believe it was at that exact moment I became aware of the doormat status of women.

It was also at that time that World War II offered women a new status. With the men off to war women were called upon, not only to build ships and weapons, but to run businesses and maintain a home as well. Add to that the sense of self-worth that comes with a paycheck, and you see the dawn of a revolution.

When the men returned after the war, I headed for college, a woman's college, no less! It was the College of St. Benedict in Minnesota, and it was a World Without Men, Amen! There I was witness to the good sisters who did it all in war and peace. They were the farmers that drove tractors and harvested crops, mended fences, baked and preserved foods, and earned Ph.D.s, taught school and wrote books. There I learned that women are smart, strong, compassionate, and wise. We can do anything!

That didn't prevent us from getting married, though, when Mr. Right came along, even if it was at The Wrong Time. For me it was in the middle of my sophomore year, when I naively convinced myself that marriage would never prevent me from writing. Maybe so, but having babies every year sure put a cramp in my style.

Benedictine training to the rescue! I taught my children about the nobility of work while I taught them to clean, cook, and baby-sit. Spurred on by Betty Friedan's *Feminine Mystique* and the women's movement of the sixties, (to say nothing of the need for money to feed and clothe our brood) I returned to school. Bob and the kids pitched in, and even though I had to get up at 4 a.m. to write papers and study, work in the theater department to help pay my tuition, and do all the laundry and cooking at home, it was worth it.

With all ten kids, Bob, my mother, sisters and Aunt Helen in attendance, I had a great cheering section at my graduation. Bob's eyes were sparkling with dollar signs because I had signed a teaching contract, but Aunt Helen didn't notice. She offered a toast at the party afterwards, "To Bob, who really deserves all the credit," she said in her typical 30s mentality, "Because he allowed his wife to go back to school."

Gail Sheehy offers good news to women in her *The Silent Passage*. She points out that women often become more aggressive and goal-oriented after menopause, exhibiting more of a take-charge attitude., thanks to an increase in the male hormone, testosterone. Think of the consequences of that! When our daughters, with better educations, fewer children, and many more years in the work force, finally are post-menopausal, they will take their rightful places running the country as well as the Fortune 500.

I can just hear their voices raised with that woman in the cartoon, "So watch your step!"

I'VE DONE THAT!

As I flipped through the yellow pages recently, looking for a wallpaper and painting service, I couldn't help wallowing in the pleasure of it all. Time was when I would have had to read up on the technique, buy or borrow all the equipment, then struggle valiantly with my amateur skills in an effort to do the job like a pro. One of the great rewards of reaching the age of mature wisdom is the ability to say, "Let's have George do it. I've done that."

My friend, Pat, says she has a list that grows longer each day. It's her "I've-done-that-list." During all those years of living hand-to-mouth, if we wanted anything beyond the bare necessities, we did it ourselves. Some of our skills, such as sewing, were finally polished enough to create winter coats and bridal gowns. And our canning was impressive. We could dazzle the eye of any beholder with row upon row of quart jars stored for the winter: golden peaches, ruby red tomatoes, purple plums, like jewels gleaming in our basement. We tiled floors, hung miles of wallpaper, taped plasterboard seams, and rolled and brushed gallons of paint. In our exuberance for home improvements, we were willing to settle for less than perfect. What choice did we have?

When I went shopping for a husband, I had a list of requirements that read "brilliant, handsome, good Catholic, witty, and kind." It never occurred to me to include "handy," however, so Bob filled the bill nicely. He grew up as the son of a cabinet maker, who wouldn't let him touch a tool. "Stick to your books!" he'd admonish him. "You'll never be worth a damn with your hands!" Combine that kind of husband with a wife who is brimming with enthusiasm, self-confidence, and wild creativity, and you have a recipe for disaster.

The first time we wallpapered a room was one such experience. We had purchased our first home, a very old home, where the former owner had paneled all of the downstairs rooms with beautiful knotty pine, but did our bedroom upstairs in a gray asphalt tile (yes, roofing material!) in an attempt to create an outdoor garden effect. It was here that he could entertain clients from New York while his two maiden sisters sweat buckets in the kitchen below, cooking up "Sister's Home Style Salad Dressing." (A picture of our home's exterior appeared on the labels.) After a year in that dreary bedroom, I could stand it no longer and decided to wallpaper over the gritty asphalt tile in my typical manner: zeal exceeding common sense.

Bob, of course, said it couldn't be done, but what did he know? I accepted his negative attitudes as yet another challenge, and set to work while he was off playing a dance job. (He taught by day and drummed by night.) Each strip that went up thrilled me more as I watched the room go from dark and dreary to bright and cheery. I was putting up the final strip when Bob returned home at 2 a.m. Seeing his appreciative smile was half the fun. As we climbed happily into bed, he asked, "What's that crackling sound?" I assured him it was probably the sound wallpaper makes when it's drying. In my exhausted state I went happily to sleep to the soothing sound of paper drying. Snap, crackle pop!

I awoke a few hours later to the light touch of paper wrapping us up in our beds. Whole sheets had fallen upon us! We lay buried in our paper tomb. As we fought our way out and tripped over more sheets on the floor, we were able to laugh at my foolishness, and to remind ourselves that this is why paper hangers can charge so much. They know better than to attempt the impossible.

Some people need to learn the same lesson over and over. I'm one of them. My next brain-storm was for laying tile in the front hall. I was amazed to learn how cheaply we could buy the materials and do it ourselves. I listened with rapt wonder as the tile salesman explained the simple way to transform our dreary hallway into a brilliant, elegant foyer. I trudged home lugging the heavy tiles, filled with visions of beautiful, gleaming floors I would create by following these simple instructions: Start with a clean floor, spread the black goo liberally over entire surface, measure to find the center, then carefully lay out the tiles in the desired pattern, starting in the center. Press down and wipe away the black stuff as it oozes up between the tiles. Bob agreed to help, since I was eight months pregnant and we were assured, "Anyone could do it!"

We started after tucking the kids into bed at 8 p.m. and by 10 we had already realized it was a lot more work than we expected. No one told us to go easy on the black goo. We figured more was better, so the darn stuff kept oozing between cracks, and we kept wiping and wiping *ad infinitum*. I think the obstruction I carried in front prevented me from seeing the working area as I crawled around on all fours. By 3 a.m. we were not half finished, and I feared going into labor in this exhausted state. I smudged my face with black goo each time I wiped away my tears. And there, at the opposite end of the hall was my husband, seething with anger, bellowing, "What in God's name am I doing here? I am not a tile layer! I am a philosopher!" With that we summoned just enough energy to laugh and drag ourselves to bed.

We ended up paying someone to straighten our mess. Still, I would continue to try such things over and over for the next 30 years. Eventually I acquired some skills, and some efforts paid off, but even those jobs I could do acceptably well lost their luster for me as I grew older.

Bob and I have acquired the greatest respect for craftsmen who enter our home with their confident strides and their well-used tools. We are happy to pay the price they demand, and we stand in awe at the grace and ease with which they move.

"Let George do it!" we say now, without the slightest tinge of guilt as we buy our ready-made clothes and hire our painters and paper hangers. After all, we don't have to prove ourselves any longer. We've done that!

It's just one of the delightful surprises we've found in the pot at the end of the rainbow. Freedom!

CHURCH

WITH A HEART

IS AFTER

MY OWN

CHURCH WITH A HEART IS AFTER MY OWN

Pope John XXIII made history when he opened some windows in the church during Vatican II. Although that was more than thirty years ago, and the clergy crept slowly into these changes, some of the "old" Catholics are still resisting the pressure to change. For those of us who have made the effort to digest the innovations, however, the rewards are tremendous. Today's Church appears to be more like a loving mother than the stern disciplinarian I remember from my childhood.

Much of the talk of sin and punishment, rules and restrictions, has been replaced with gestures of love and understanding. Today's Catholic Church feels like a church with a heart, and it appears that the world's bishops are achieving the "kinder, gentler society" that President Bush only dreamed about in his campaign rhetoric of the 80s.

While we were being told that we must attend Sunday Mass under pain of mortal sin, we were not made to feel welcome as we are today. The priest (host) came out of his private confines, and with his back to the congregation recited prayers in a foreign language, and he was answered by small servers in the same tongue. A communion rail further separated us from the ceremony, in which we were little more than spectators. No wonder everyone else was busy doing his own thing! Several old ladies were mumbling over their beads, some were praying a novena, some planning what they'd have for dinner tonight or, in the case of younger people at least, wondering why they were required to be here. What did any of this foreign stuff have to do with them and their world?

They didn't have to wonder for long, because with the homily came their weekly dose of "fire and brimstone." Because missing Mass on Sunday was a mortal sin, that's why! And everyone knew what a mortal sin meant: Die with one and you're damned! To a kid in the 30s or 40s, this meant if you planned on committing one you'd better CYA! You did this by building up a big savings account of indulgences through "ejaculations" (that's little prayers, for the information of youngsters under 45) or visiting the Church when you didn't have to, or sacrificing candy during Lent!

When I hear Catholics grumble about how much holier the nuns were when "nuns were nuns" and everyone knew it, I get the message, "Why should they wear ordinary clothes when those scratchy wool habits and stiff coifs binding their necks set them apart from the rest of us?" So I like to point out that the church is both kinder and tougher with religious at the same time. The clothing may be more comfortable, but the challenge is greater. They have to get our respect the old fashioned way; they *earn* it with their deeds instead of their duds!

I can never attend a wedding or funeral in a Protestant Church these days without recalling my mother crying over my cousin's wedding. She was married in a Protestant church, and our pastor would not permit Mother to attend. It would seem to condone it. Today more consideration is given to loving kindness.

And how about the Catholic marrying a non-Catholic with a priest officiating? Was it necessary to restrict the ceremony to the rectory instead of the church? And forever after be labeled "mixed marriage." The Catholic spouse and all the friends and relatives inside the fold would storm heaven with prayers to "save the soul" of the non-Catholic by allowing him or her to see the light and be converted. We still want the non-Catholic partner to join our fold, of course, but we avoid the implication that there is no salvation for him if he doesn't.

Then there are (God forbid!) divorced Catholics. Most of us "seniors" can recall several who remained in abusive relationships rather than divorce. Some hung on doggedly after divorce, regularly attending Sunday Mass, even though they were barred from sacraments, but far more took one look at their "lower class" status and walked away forever.

Today the Catholic newly-divorced are treated, along with the newly-widowed, with the compassion they deserve. Support groups abound in nearly every parish community throughout the diocese. These groups recognize the heartache and the trauma of ended relationships, and strive to help these wounded, grieving people become whole again by restoring rather than robbing their dignity.

Little by little, following Vatican II in the 60s, we came to realize that morality and love of your fellow man were not the exclusive domain of Catholics. We discovered some wonderfully good followers of Christ in other churches. Ecumenism was the balm that healed many old festering wounds. When a priest friend of ours was a guest lecturer at a Lutheran conference, he confided to us that he prayed and grieved over past sins against charity that we had committed in the name of Catholicism.

Gradually, as we introduced the responses in English, the handshake of peace, the laymen as lectors and Eucharistic Ministers, and the presentation of gifts from the congregation, the word spread among laymen: We belong. We celebrate the Eucharist. It is not a church of the clergy after all, but a church owned and operated by all practicing Catholics. *We are the church!*

The clergy are the ordained ministers of the sacraments, but it is the duty of the laity to become informed and then to use our God-given talents for our church. So if things aren't going the way we'd like, guess who is responsible?

Why would anyone want to go back to the old ways? We Catholics have finally begun to understand the message of Love that Christ preached through his entire ministry, His death on the cross, and His redemption.

Why, in God's holy name, did it take 21 centuries to figure it out?

GOD'S HUMOR
SLAYS ME

O ne of the most valuable lessons I ever learned in my fourteen years of Catholic education was that God has a sense of humor. I remember Sister Gregory (a Franciscan teaching at Madonna High School in Aurora, Illinois) telling us with a grin that she always saw God's humor in popcorn. What a delightful image that evokes: God designing an ear of corn and saying, "Wait 'till they see what happens when they drop these kernels into a hot pan!"

This idea can be extended into the entire act of creation. Like a gentle father hiding Easter eggs, He went about hiding penicillin in mold. ("Ha! Ha! Wait till they discover what was right under their noses all along!") milk in cows' udders (the prototype for spigots of all kinds), and heating oil buried deep enough in the earth that man had to first design some fancy equipment to get at it.

Ah, yes! The Master Teacher employed the inductive method and made sure there were plenty of challenges to force us to work together and keep us occupied for centuries.

Looking back at the Old Testament we find entire comedy plots worthy of the best script writers. God's humor is evident in His ordering of Noah to build an arc in the desert, one of the earliest "Fools for God" (No, Bill Cosby didn't just dream that up). And then there's Jonah, of course. Jonah rejects God's command to go teach the Ninevites. He argues that he doesn't have the talent for it, when in fact, he doesn't have the stomach for it, plain and simple. He disliked the Ninevites intensely. So he stole away on board a ship to get out of the assignment, and what does God do? He sends a storm that tosses Jonah into the sea. Like a smart parent, the Lord decides what Jonah needs is some time out to ponder his behavior. He then has him swallowed by a whale, no less, who after giving Jonah many long days and nights of pondering time in his dark belly, spits him out on the shores of Nineveh. Boy, did those Ninevites look good to him!

In my own life I have always been aware of God's humor, sometimes painfully so. When Bob and I got married at 19 and 20, we had a combined total of 26 years of Catholic education between us, and thought we knew it all. Those poor suckers in public schools were going to have to limp along, but we would march boldly forward armed with The Truth. "I'd like to have thirteen children," I often spouted off in my most righteous manner.

What I knew about children could have been put in a penny Guess What Book. I had baby-sat once or twice and didn't enjoy it in the least, and my older sisters had no children, so how was I to know? Bob had two years left to complete his undergraduate degree, but no problem. Learn the Rhythm Method!

Remember God's humor? Does He ever have fun with that one! Despite the song to the contrary, not all God's chillun got rhythm. I kept telling God, quietly at first, and finally screaming it, "I was only kidding when I said 13, Lord! You know we aren't equipped to handle any more. Financially! Emotionally! We're likely to ruin the entire batch. Now cut it out!" Every newly discovered pregnancy was greeted with tears, but when the babies finally waved their little fists in the air and looked into our eyes we were a lot like Jonah, whispering, "Thanks, Lord. It's just what I wanted." There were no planned pregnancies, but no unwanted babies either.

A few years ago, while teaching, I walked into a discussion of family planning in progress in the faculty lounge. Knowing I had ten children, someone cleverly drew me into the conversation by asking, "Well, Audrey, how many of your children were planned?" The question stumped me. I had never given it any thought until then, but recalling that the first one arrived fourteen months after our marriage and wasn't paid for until well into the third or fourth pregnancy, I had to admit, "None." They, of course, found this hilarious and gave it their heartiest thigh-slapping laughter. I'm always happy to provide a little humor for my fellow teachers.

But God's humor is different. There is no malice in it. Despite the fact that I cried out from time to time, "Lord, I don't think you're funny!" I really do see it now. My worst fear was that we'd "ruin the whole batch" because we couldn't fill their needs. But looking at them today and admiring their achievements in the market place and in the helping professions, their levels of education, their parenting skills, and the love they show to us and to one another, I can see that we had a lot of help from an Unseen Partner with an indestructible sense of humor.

It sure took Him long enough to get to the punch line, though.

A TALE OF TWO BENNIES

When the subject of religious vocations arises, you may notice a far away look in my eyes and just the slightest touch of a smirk settling about my lips. That's because I am recalling my own vocation story, which I call "A Tale of Two Bennies."

Once upon a time, two young ladies enrolled as freshmen at the College of St. Benedict in Minnesota. This made them Bennies. They lived in the same dorm, loved the same kinds of literature and theater, and had meals and classes together. This made them good friends, despite their differences. One was filled with dreams and the other was filled with God. And when they strolled along the wooded paths after dinner, the one filled with dreams would talk about becoming a great actress or writing The Great Catholic Novel. And her God-filled friend was joyful, witty, and responsive. She praised her friend's acting in the college productions and her writing efforts in the college literary magazine. But she laughed when her friend made little things for her hope chest. "Potholders! Why would anyone waste her time on such trivialities?"

When they returned as sophomores, the dreamer had a shock. She found her friend waiting on tables, wearing the uniform of a postulant. She had joined the convent! She would take the vows of poverty, chastity, and obedience. Oh, no! How could she? Now their paths would lead them far apart. Within a year each of them would assume a new identity. One would become Sister Colman O'Connell, O.S.B. and the other would be Mrs. Robert Fixmer, the dreamer who scorned Poverty, Chastity and Obedience, but had little more than those few potholders.

When I married Bob, this former seminarian with a major in Catholic philosophy, we gloated over how well prepared we were to raise a good family. All that great background in Catholic literature and Catholic philosophy! How could we go wrong? So I didn't know how to cook and he didn't know how to use a hammer. Big deal!

The readers of this column are familiar with some of the hurdles Bob and I leaped in our race for survival: Trying to work with the Rhythm Method until finally we blocked weeks off the calendar each month! Feeding the Hungry without benefit of multiplying loaves and fishes! Clothing the Naked without suffocating in diapers and unmated socks! Bearing Wrongs Patiently when asked, "But why would you have more children than you can afford?"

Once I returned to St. Ben's to visit my friend, Dee, or as I soon learned, Sr. Colman Ph.D. (from the Catholic University. . .in theater). She escorted Bob and me and our throng of children around their new three million dollar theater, where she was department chair. I "oohed and aahed" so much over this dream-come-true that my daughter later asked, "Mama, is your friend really rich?" And, of course, I hugged her closely and said truthfully, "No, dear, we are the ones who are rich."

But I asked myself, what's wrong with this picture? Who took the vows of poverty, chastity, and obedience? Is poverty getting a first class education, living and working in beautiful surroundings but just not owning anything? Or is it living hand-to-mouth with the awesome responsibility of feeding, clothing, and educating a big family? Is chastity sleeping alone? Or is it sleeping beside someone you love but mustn't touch? Is obedience allowing a mother superior to design your career? Or is it allowing God to plan your family? Can't we honestly say that a good Catholic marriage is a religious vocation, too?

Five years ago, after finally earning a couple of degrees myself and having 20 years of teaching behind me, I returned to St. Ben's, this time for the inauguration of Sister Colman as President of the College of St. Benedict. She looked smashing in her designer suit, her light touch of cosmetics and jewelry, and her trim figure, thanks to being a marathon runner. The academic procession of college presidents from all over the nation and their splendid tributes to the new president were awesome. And seeing the mansion that was now hers as president, I understood that it was fitting. After all, she must entertain dignitaries from all walks of life. So material rewards do come to religious as well as laity for jobs well done.

Recently I was moved by another procession: the priests of the Madison Diocese at the Holy Week Chrism Mass. It was both touching and frightening , this long, gray line. Where are the young ones? Who will be left to serve our spiritual needs in 20 years? The laymen, of course. The hopeful note was Bishop Bullock's evident pastoral qualities. His warm recognition of the priestly strengths and his efforts to meet and greet the laymen created a strong feeling of community and caring.

Caring! That would seem to be our most urgent obligation. Caring for the few priests and sisters we have. Caring enough to say, "Thanks for that inspiring homily!" as we leave church. Caring enough to lighten their already double load by asking, "What can I do?" (We seniors have the time and talent to do much more!) Caring enough to bite our tongues rather than criticize, and enough to open our hearts and homes to these lonely people shifting and cooking for themselves.

Who knows? We might even inspire new vocations by simply showing greater respect and appreciation for our overworked religious. It's worth a try, isn't it?

PAPA'S HERE

E arly in the week of August 9, 1993, the city of Denver didn't exactly appear to be rolling out the red carpet for its distinguished Vatican Visitor. It seemed more like a tiny kingdom gearing up for an invasion of Huns. Denverites, weary of the year-long plans to close off streets and put in a supply of water to sustain life, were making plans to flee the city *en masse*. *As* they traveled to and from work on I-25, they encountered signs that warned with flashing lights, "Papal Mass on August 15. Expect delays!" At the Cherry Creek Reservoir, "Dam Road closed from noon August 14 to 4 p.m. August 15."

Neighborhoods nearby even issued passes to allow residents to enter their streets and park near their own homes.

In my daughter Elizabeth's neighborhood each homeowner found a message on shocking pink paper taped to their front door. Headlined "Disaster Preparedness," this bulletin carried instructions for securing their property: the area would be policed by volunteers throughout the day and night, extra lighting was installed around the swimming pools, and each home should keep outdoor lights burning. Someone would man the Disaster Hot Line around the clock for residents to report anything suspicious. It made me so nervous that I considered removing the World Youth Day Press Pass I was wearing around my neck and substituting it with a sign that said, "I'm okay. My daughter lives here."

Elizabeth was concerned about all of the negative vibes she was picking up. When she dropped her dog off on Thursday morning at her friend Jean's house, she emerged shaking her head. "Most of the neighbors are leaving town, but Jean and Jim feel they have to stay for their watch duty. They aren't Catholic and they think this is crazy. Jean was really impressed by the kids she saw on TV at the opening Mass last night, though. By the way, she saw you too, right up there in front."

On Thursday night when Elizabeth picked up her dog, she found the couple glued to the TV set. "We've been watching every moment since his arrival. Imagine the pope and the President both right here in Denver!" They thought sadly of the neighbors who had fled the city. "Boy, they don't know what they're missing!"

TV anchors were running a marathon of stories. Frequently heard were such things as, "This is incredibly moving. You sure don't have to be Catholic to appreciate this."

If there were protest groups in the city, they failed to attract the media. Nothing short of the appearance of Christ Himself could have detracted from the spectacle of 160,000 youths from 70 nations gathering to proclaim their faith, feed their souls, and pay tribute to the Vicar of Christ on earth.

With the arrival of Pope John Paul II, all differences were forgotten. No more interviews with nuns who wanted to be ordained, Catholics who wanted to dump *Humanae Vitae,* or abortion rights activists. *The Denver Post* ran a banner headline, "Hope and History" and another "Sea of Love Washes Over Pope at Mile High." *The Rocky Mountain News* shouted, "Pope's Message Rocks Stadium." And on the final days, "Youths, Pope Leave Coloradans Charmed," and "Four Days to Touch the Heart." It was a media love blitz to behold!

One Catholic I know put it this way. "I came here just lukewarm about this pope. I totally disagree with his views on contraception, but now that I see his charisma, the way he uses the modern media to bring people to a spiritual awareness, I don't know. Maybe he is the right man for the job after all."

A cab I was riding in pulled up alongside a car with an obviously irritated driver at the wheel. He was scowling because we had to wait while a group of perhaps a hundred kids crossed the street. I watched the scowl turned to a smile, then a grin as the kids waved cheerily at us, and "God-blessed" us all over the place. The cab driver exclaimed, "These are the best and the brightest kids in the world right here in Denver."

I spoke to a police officer on Monday morning who said that not a single incident of crime had been reported among these World Youth Day participants. The only problem they created for them was the medical treatments for dehydration, blisters, and such things.

And neighbor Jean? Her only complaint was that darn watch duty. It was dreadfully boring. She could have been inside watching every minute of the pope's visit on TV.

With great fatigue and more than a little regret, we watched Al Gore and his young son seeing John Paul off on Sunday night.

Monday morning a touch of nostalgia permeated the *Denver Post* with its lead article beginning, "It was a custom at one time to give a visiting dignitary a key to the city. Pope John Paul II didn't need a key. They gave him the city." And the headline, "Arrivederci Papa," used the more familiar Italian term for the pope to suggest that we, all of us, had been warmed by his love, and had come to feel the profound and comforting joy of his embrace.

Arrivederci, Papa!

PARDON ME, YOUR HAIR SHIRT IS SHOWING

We seem to slide into Holy Week more gracefully these days. Maybe it's because more priests emphasize the spiritual journey through Lent, and more Catholics seem to be doing something positive, like attending daily Mass, where symbols which anticipate new life are everywhere. In our church, for example, five large paper mache cocoons hang on a tree, rather ugly cocoons from which we may expect beautiful butterflies to emerge on Easter, This is a nice reminder that God isn't finished with us yet. And God alone knows how beautiful we might be when we emerge from our cocoon of sin. (I've requested an Elizabeth Taylor-type face, if that pattern is still available.)

But what gets Lent off to a good start is the reading we get from Matthew soon after Ash Wednesday. In it we are warned not to advertise our suffering for the whole world to see.

"When you fast, do not look somber as the hypocrites do, for they disfigure their faces to show men they are fasting. I tell you the truth they have received their reward in full, but when you fast put oil on your face so that it will not be obvious to men that you are fasting. . .and your father who sees what is done in secret will reward you." (Matt. 6/16-18)

Of course, today that needs to be modified to read, "Style your hair, wash your face, and put on your makeup." I know in my case if I went forth into the market place without make-up, I would be forcing the penance on others, and I'd appear to be suffering more than I actually was, thereby missing the point completely.

I wonder if that reading was unknown when I was younger. I'm sure my relatives never heard it. Take my Aunt Mildred, a.k.a. "The Pillar of St. Hedwigs." It seemed to me she powdered her face with flour during Lent, and she was always dropping her 300 pound bulk into the nearest chair and feigning weakness from "all that dreadful fasting." I suspect she'd find a subtle way to get around those words of Matthew even today. She'd no doubt go for the layered look, with the cuffs of her hair shirt poking out of her blouse.

But then everyone talked about their sacrifices. Come Ash Wednesday and "Hi, how are you?" was replaced with, "What are you giving up for Lent?" We didn't have a lot of choices in those days during the Depression. There was no TV, and the dime you spent on the movies could buy a can of Kroger's Tall Boy soup, enough to feed a whole family.

Candy was about the only luxury, so candy it was. Everyone gave up candy. A penny earned was a penny spent on a B-B Bat sucker or two jaw-breakers, hard little balls with a burst of nutty goodness that rewarded the patient all-day sucker. If you happened to be visited by a rich uncle, of course, you might have an entire nickel to spend. With that you could buy a big Snickers bar, a long tube of Necco wafers, or my all-time favorite, Three Musketeers.

When I was eight and my sister, Mary Lou, was six, Mother got the idea of monitoring our penance by having us save every piece of candy that came our way. Mary Lou bawled and carried on so Mama said she could be excused since she was only six and hadn't "reached the age of reason." Most Catholics didn't even have candy around during Lent. And if you saw someone about to embark upon a Hershey bar, let's say, you felt compelled to remind him.

A Protestant neighbor of ours, however, often rewarded me for running to the store for her with a piece of her luscious homemade fudge. This I dutifully handed over to Mother to wrap in waxed paper and store for me 'till Holy Saturday. That year every penny I got was spent on B-B Bats or jaw-breakers, but I carried them home in sticky hands and stashed them into a shoe-box of my father's, which I had optimistically selected. I barely had the bottom covered, but when a Holloway sucker found its way into the box, I knew that my Sweet Easter was assured. I became obsessed with watching my sweet cache grow, wringing my hands with wicked glee each time Mother brought out the box for me to add another piece. I fantasized about the end of Lent when I could, at long last, savor the rewards of my noble martyrdom.

Unfortunately, Mary Lou, who had not yet developed a conscience, was spying on us when we stashed the box away. When at last Holy Saturday came and we returned from the long morning at church, Mama brought down my box and I burst into tears. My beautiful collection was almost gone! Mary Lou, with her six -year-old conscience and her twenty-year-old cunning, denied it at first. But how else could two out of three Musketeers escape? Who else could have sucked all the color out of the jaw-breakers, leaving only the white ball with blue dots behind? Do mice unwrap fudge or carry off a Holloway sucker?

Finally my little sister admitted the foul deed, and with a toss of her curly head and her big blue eyes upturned in an innocent gaze, she exclaimed, "But I haven't reached the age of reason!"

I have hated that phrase ever since, finding that reason is a relative thing, and some of my relatives never did reach it right up to the day they died.

The nuns in high school had the right idea. They always said, "You don't have to give up things; do something positive." Going to daily Mass during Lent seemed just right, especially after I married and had kids of my own. And unlike saving up my candy, the rewards of Daily Mass were built in. It was a heckuva lot more peaceful in church than at home, where 10 kids were getting ready for school, fighting over who was wearing whose clothes. It was my oasis in the desert, my manna from heaven. By the time I returned to the battleground, serene and refreshed, I could pack their lunches and see them off without screaming at them.

Church had the same effect as washing the face in biblical times. No one dreamed I was making a sacrifice, not even me!

NEW LOOK IN
CONFESSIONS

A sure cure for the "Catholic Guilt" of which we are supposedly ridden, would seem to be daytime television. Recently Bob and I were watching one of those Never-Ending Problems shows. You know the kind, where Sally or Oprah or Phil dig deep into the dregs of society to unearth these creatures who murdered a spouse, abused a child, cheated a boss, or cross-dressed for weekend sport? That day Sally had drawn out a particularly immoral guest with such skill that the more the sinner exposed himself, the more the audience jeered him.

"Why would anyone want to confess their sins to millions of viewers?" asked my husband.

"I don't know," I said, "But do you suppose all these public confessions have destroyed our desire to confess to the priest?"

That little exchange started me thinking about the sweeping changes that we senior citizens have seen since Vatican II. From the stylized formula "Confession" of the thirties, to the freer "Rite of Reconciliation" today, our generation had a mixed reaction. A few went along, some stubbornly insisted on entering the dark little box, and others who were once regulars stayed away completely.

An example is a story told by a friend of mine, who had convinced herself that she was living in a state of grace, receiving the Eucharist every day through most of the year, and, consequently, in no need of "reconciliation." Every time her husband went to Confession she brushed it off with a confident, I-don't-need-it attitude. She was curious, however, about the new Rite of Reconciliation that was being offered in a nearby community, so one day she said to her husband, "I think that's one of those deals where you get a group absolution." Fifty for the price of one? Wow! Always with an eye for a bargain, she added, " Let's go."

As it turned out, it was more than she bargained for. Three priests strode to the altar fully vested. The rite started out nicely with one of the priests reading some inspirational words from the scriptures, and that was okay, pleasant and non-threatening enough. But then in a flash the three priests scattered to their corners like boxers in a ring, and lo and behold! Everyone in the congregation was out of their pews in three lines like lambs to the slaughter.

My friend was horrified. They were going to confess individually? Standing out there in broad daylight they were going to confess their sins to the priest? No way would she get trapped into one of those lineups! She felt tricked and angry at first, but as her husband worked his way through one of the long lines she had plenty of time to cool down. Words began to formulate in her mind. She should march right up there and tell that priest how she felt about Confession. Just tell him she considers herself an "insider" already. What's to be reconciled? When one line shrank to two people remaining, she bolted out of her seat and joined it, her folded arms expressing her determination not to be tricked into giving one of those old formula confessions.

My friend told this story to a group of us, who found it so amusing that we were laughing hysterically, but she was dead serious. "So I walked up to that priest and he shook hands with me and smiled warmly. Can you beat that? But I let him have it anyway. I said, 'I hope this won't shock you, but I haven't been to confession in four years.' And guess what he said? 'That's no problem.' I nearly fainted! So then I told him I didn't have any serious sins. At my age, what can you do? Get mad at your husband, stretch the truth a little, that kind of thing. But God is my friend already. Why do I need reconciliation? And you know, he was wonderful. He didn't argue. He just smiled, placed his hand on my head, blessed me and said, 'I absolve you.' And you know what's really weird about it? I felt wonderful!"

Now I wanted to learn more about the New Rite, so I checked out a few books on the subject from Bob's vast library, and found one particularly enlightening. It was *The Theology of Penance* by Hebblethwaite and Donovan, S.J., published by Clergy Book Service. It describes the evolvement of confession in three stages.

In the early church there was Canonical Penance that dealt only with the most grievous sins like murder, apostasy and adultery, and could only be given once in a lifetime. Tariffed Penance was next, and each sin carried a specific penance or tariff, but another important difference was that it could be repeated. Modern Penance, a form distinguished by the granting of absolution before the penance is carried out, emerged gradually in the twelfth century. The rite itself, however, changed little in the next eight centuries.

Vatican II took a new look at sin. Two things struck me in the chapter on "New Thinking of Sin": the revolution in our concept of sin (a new awareness of catastrophic social sins like nuclear bombs, malnutrition, exploitation of classes, as opposed to individuals breaking the laws of God) and how the new sciences of psychology, sociology and anthropology broadened our understanding of the role of environment in shaping a person's character and moral outlook. This insight is recognized by a new theology, which emphasizes the communal nature of sin. We sin against God when we sin against man.

Imagine that! If we sin against man (communal sin) then confession and forgiveness must also be communal acts. So the "Never-Ending Problems" shows on TV might be filling a need after all? By acknowledging the wrongs he or she did to society or to an individual a person may be reconciled? But the guests on Oprah's or Phil's shows aren't always sorry, are they?

No one is foolish enough to think that a TV talk show could replace the sacrament, but I can see how this confessing, purging, and examining choices to remedy the problems, could be valuable. Under the guidance of a qualified professional psychiatrist, psychotherapist, or other expert, millions of people are learning how to recognize and change their behaviors (sins, if you will.)

In the introduction to *The New Rite* we read, "Penance always entails reconciliation with our brothers and sisters who are always harmed by our sins." Maybe we should follow the ancient Ukrainian custom. Before receiving the sacrament, they travel from neighbor to neighbor making peace with those they have offended, and *then* they seek God's forgiveness. Not a bad idea!

TAKING CHRISTMAS
OUT OF CHRISTMAS

I n the early 1950s Bob was teaching English in a public high school in a small community that was predominantly Catholic. He won the hearts of all these good Catholic farmers and businessmen with a Christmas program he wrote, directed, and narrated. The full band and chorus of exuberant teenagers participated to make this an exciting extravaganza. The theme was one that was just beginning to grow in popularity: Put Christ back into Christmas.

Today we look back with a sense of awe that Bob should have been able to pull this off in a public school. Soon after I began teaching, in the early '70s, I developed a unit designed to stop fighting the Christmas spirit that was pulling the kids from their studies of language and literature all through the month of December, and instead channel that energy into a production of essays, speeches, and literature on the subject uppermost in their minds: Christmas.

The theme was nothing so blatantly religious as putting Christ back into Christmas, mind you, but merely a celebration of the Christmas Spirit, and a celebration of our differences of traditions and customs. Students used all of their communication skills to express their emotions: disappointment when they learned about Santa, anticipation of harnessing "the big one," the fun of joining in family affairs.

In an effort to bring these adolescents out of their typical self-centered mode, I had them each write a letter to Santa asking for something for someone else, someone they knew who was suffering or needy in one way or another. "Think of Santa as having the powers of God for this purpose. He can make people well, work miracles of all kinds," I would tell them, in an effort to safely avoid religious overtones. Only once or twice in all those years did a student say, "Why can't I just write a letter to God?" and then I would happily bestow my blessing.

Since I did not allow them to write in generalities, but required them to write about a specific person, however, I most often ran into the objection, "I don't know anyone who is suffering."

"Then look around you. Put yourself in others' shoes. Walk around in their skin. How do you feel? What do you long for? Use fictitious names if you wish, but write about real people."

Most of my students were Christians who celebrated Christmas. But wherever we encountered a Jewish person or a Jehovah's Witness, I encouraged them to share their customs with us, and I made it clear that never would they be forced to do anything that was in contradiction to their religion. The result was an exciting variety of essays and speeches in which Catholic students demonstrated Advent wreaths, Jewish students brought in a menorah to explain Hanukkah, and Jehovah's Witnesses explained why they didn't celebrate Christmas. It was a delightful smorgasbord of customs!

Over a period of 20 years I developed and perfected this unit, building some precious memories and a nice collection of notes from both parents and students, praising the unit for helping the entire family celebrate the true spirit of Christmas. It made the language lessons that much more enjoyable, to say nothing of more worthwhile.

Imagine my surprise, then, to learn that Christmas had become a dirty word. It was in the last year of my teaching,

1990, that I was called into the principal's office to get my warning. "We must abide by the law," he said with a touch of sadness, "so you will have to discontinue any mention of Christmas. If you can go through all your materials and change the word to Holiday you'll be okay. Just don't mention Christmas again."

I thanked him politely and said it was a good thing I was planning to retire anyway. I didn't think the unit would be the same without Christmas. Besides, in a few years they'll probably ban the word holiday. Sounds too much like holy day, and God forbid (whoops! I mean Heaven forbid? No, Clinton forbid?) Anyway, we don't want to offend the atheists, now do we?

Parochial schools are looking better all the time.

NO PLACE LIKE HOME CHURCH

Being a Catholic has certain membership privileges for the traveler. It's like some spiritual health club where you're guaranteed facilities in which to work out your spiritual muscles in nearly every city in the world. Your rosary should be like that American Express card. Don't leave home without it. And what a comfort to know that millions of clergymen are standing by to take your emergency call around the clock. Just like the trusty old AT&T operators. Such security!

As the kids grew up and I finally emerged from the kitchen, I wanted to keep going further and further, and that's when I came to appreciate the security that my membership in the Church offered. Because whether we're in Fairfield Bay, Arkansas or in Paris, France, the Eucharist is celebrated with the same familiar reverence as it is back home in Wisconsin. We should borrow that slogan spouted by McDonald's (Ramada Inn? Hardee's?) Anyway, the chain that advertised, "The best surprise is no surprise." When you're feeling foreign phobia, it's such a comfort to find you "fit" in a Catholic Church.

Of course, there are some exceptions to that Church security. On one memorable occasion we visited a magnificent old cathedral in Seattle. As we waited for Mass to begin I noticed the rather noisy entry of a woman into the pew behind us. She was dressed shabbily with what appeared to be a dish towel draped loosely over her head to shield her from the heavy rain, no doubt. As the priest ascended the pulpit and began preaching, we were startled by a loud voice behind us grumbling, "I can't take this any more. It's all lies." The homily stopped. We sat transfixed as she began screaming, "You are the anti-Christ! You are evil!" as the ushers led her, kicking and screaming, out the door.

In the stunned silence that followed, the priest said something about being criticized for allowing the homeless the use of the church and then resumed his homily. It was not until we got up to leave, that we realized Bob's cap was no longer in the pew. In its place was the soggy dishtowel the lady had worn. As my gracious spouse grumbled and groused about the fate of his hat, I reminded him that it probably gave that poor creature great satisfaction to return to her street friends proudly wearing his grey tweed cap. "Yeah," grumbled Bob, "And by now she has traded it for a bottle of cheap wine!" So much for security in the big city churches.

It was at our son's church this Christmas, however, where we learned that even the familiar can be unfamiliar. Now, we've always loved the lively spirit in these Denver churches. If I feel at all out of place it's only because the average age of the congregation seems to be slightly below 35, and the priests sound like graduates of the Billy Graham school of preaching with Ph.D.'s in multi-media to boot. Tim warned us that his church is so crowded that if you don't get there 30 minutes before Mass you must sit in one of the side rooms and watch the Mass on a TV screen. (I can do that at home!) So on Christmas Eve, allowing for even greater crowds, we arrived for the 5:30 Mass at 4:30, and settled our entire family into two rows of folding chairs.

With so much time to study the facility, questions flooded my brain. Where were the pews and kneelers? Crosses? Statues? I knew this was no Cistine Chapel, so I wasn't expecting Michelangelo when I looked up, but what were those gold drapes hanging from? Steel beams? Like the Milwaukee Airport?

"So when are you building your real church?" I asked my son.

"This is it"

No! I refused to believe it. I figured Tim wasn't really active in this parish or he would be aware of building plans. So when the priest suggested we greet the people worshipping around us (as if they hadn't been chattering nonstop for an hour already), I took the opportunity to quiz the lady behind me. No, she said, this was, indeed, the permanent church. They had done away with pews because this space was used for so many things: dances, parties, carnivals. "Even the altar platform is in sections for easy removal," she boasted. And the cross? "Oh, they will bring that in during the processional." The baptismal fountain was an enormous hunk of granite, so I figured that must be permanent. It could always double as a punch bowl, I thought, but I decided to keep the idea to myself, since my daughter had already whispered to me that my expression of disbelief was embarrassing them

Receiving Holy Communion to the beat of drums and guitars was different, but inspiring because I was surrounded by family. My euphoria quickly turned to crazy giggles, however, when at the close of Mass we were instructed to join in "Joy to the World," and the words flashed on the wall were, "Lamb of God, you take away the sins of the world." I whispered to Tim, "Is your projectionist visually impaired? Or maybe got into the punch bowl before Mass?"

I thought longingly of my home parish in Wisconsin, where our artist-in-residence had created a magnificent Christmas message, where the choir is full and extraordinary, the homilies always inspiring, and "All the children are above average." I just wanted to be like Dorothy, to click my heels together and say, "There's no place like home, there's no place like home."

But how would we really know there's no place like home unless we had been to Oz?

WHERE HAVE ALL THE CHILDREN GONE?

F allen-away-Catholics we used to call them. Today we use the softer, more generous term, "lapsed Catholics." But regardless of what they are called, we senior members of the Church feel the pain of rejection when it's our own sons and daughters in question. And if ours and our friends' experience is typical, many are praying for our kids to "come back."

When our children were small, we knew a man who disowned his daughter when she married outside the Church. Not once was she allowed to return home right up to the day he died. Fidelity is a virtue, but charity and forgiveness are even greater. I knew that as much as I loved my faith, nothing could prompt me to slam the door on my children.

We were put to the first test when the older boys were in high school, and we suspected they were skipping Sunday Mass to meet friends in a pool hall. Their irate father stormed that pool hall, and not since Christ chased the money changers out of the temple (in the Cecil B. DeMille movie, that is) did the local merchants see such a display of righteous indignation. The sticks flew, the boys fled, and the owner got the impression his business was a den of iniquity.

A priest friend advised Bob that his policy of "No Church, No Eat" was not the way to go either. And so, little by little, we had to face the reality that despite our efforts, our children were, in the end, responsible for their own souls. When they left home, we had to resign ourselves to the fact that we tried, but now they must build on that foundation, for better or worse.

Some have kept their faith and some haven't. Only one couple refused to baptize their children, stating it would be hypocritical, and the children could choose their religion when they were old enough. I thought that was as silly as saying, "I won't feed this child, but when he is hungry enough let him choose his own food." But I bit my tongue.

For many years we did what grandparents do best, we prayed. And finally Somebody Up There heard us.

In Fall I toured a famous church with some of my family. The oldest of these unbaptized children, whom I will call Danny (changing the names to protect the guilty), exclaimed, "I'm impressed with this church, Grandma!" Then in a whisper he added, "I still want to become a Catholic."

I turned up my hearing aid, asked him to repeat it, and then looked at Danny, a real hunk at 16, and already a head taller than I, and took the plunge. "Well, what are you waiting for? Your parents said they'd let you choose a religion for yourself, so are you serious ? Or is this just a whim?"

"Oh, yes, Grandma," he said. "I've looked at a lot of other religions. I've gone to churches with my friends, and read about them, and the Catholic Church is really it."

"Well, then, Danny, go for it. Tell your parents what you just told me and see what happens."

Two months later we were back for another visit, and Danny told us excitedly that he had discussed his choice with his parents, and they agreed to let him join the Church. They had no intention of going with him, however. So would Grandpa and I go with him to see the priest?

Would we! We had all we could do to keep from jumping up and hugging all of them, but we managed to appear cool as we said, "Why, of course. We'll go with you after Mass tomorrow."

The young priest received us warmly. Within minutes he set into motion the smooth operation that the Church now employs, introducing Marge, the Director of Religious Ed, a dynamic, warm, and understanding woman.

"We'd love to have you join our RCIA program, Danny. It's for adults, but there are a couple other teen-agers in it, too. We meet every Sunday night, and you won't have to decide on baptism until January. By the way, have your parents ever been baptized?"

"Oh, yes!" the three of us exclaimed in unison.

Marge didn't flinch. "I see. Well, don't worry, lots of people leave the Church for awhile. I myself left at 17 and didn't come back until I was 37. Oh, and wait 'till you get into our youth group that meets on Wednesday night. You'll love them!"

And Danny did. We soon got glowing letters from him about his sponsor. "He's a senior but he talks to me in the hall, he introduces me to all his friends, and he picks me up for RCIA." A perfect way to be initiated to a new town and school!

In January, on the feast of St. John the Baptist, Danny made his formal request in a solemn ceremony before the congregation. "My sponsor washed my feet and asked, 'What do you desire?' and I had to answer, 'I desire baptism.' And then he said, 'Why do you desire baptism?' "

"And what did you *say*, Danny?" I asked with my heart doing flip-flops.

"I said, 'Because I want God in my life.'"

I nearly cried with joy.

We could not be there for Danny's baptism, but our thoughts and prayers were with him as we participated in our own parish rite of baptism on Holy Saturday. Danny's mother bought him the gold cross and chain he wanted, and his dad took him shopping for a new suit. The snapshots they sent us show a handsome, glowing youth, whose radiant joy could not fail to inspire his younger brother and sister and the parents in attendance.

Where did Danny get the grace to make this decision? It seemed to be an innate desire, a thirst so powerful that nothing could prevent him from reaching out to the life-giving waters of baptism. Credit must also go to the moral stature of his parents, who whether they realize it or not, are products of a solid Catholic background, the living testimonials of the very faith they try to deny.

So it appears that although we may suffer lapses, hope springs eternal that the faith that drove our families for generations will be carried on after all.

Praise the Lord!

GRAND MOM: SO WHAT'S THE CATCH ?

My father taught me that nothing in this world is free; there's a price for everything. So whenever I hear another sales pitch I wait for the salesman to take a breath so I can jump in with, "Okay, so what's the catch?" The older I get the more impatient I am to get to the point. So why did it take me so many years to figure out the price of reaching senior status in the nineties?

It was in preparing my talk for the state conference of Catholic women (WCCW) that I discovered the price tag. When I looked at their theme, "If it is to be, let it be me," I asked myself what it meant. My first reaction was the rather glib, "Yeah, sure, that's what I always say, 'If you want to get the job done right, do it yourself!' "

Then I thought about the kind of women who usually appear at these things, the women of my generation, the

Veterans of the Great Rhythm Wars, who survived the Bootcamp for Sainthood as we struggled to raise big families. Today we are the silver-haired ladies whose golden voices sing out at daily Mass, "Here I am, Lord. I come to do your will."

When I heard that Bishop Wirz suggested we be recycled, I said, "Great idea! I want to come back with Liz Taylor's face and Jane Fonda's body." With a body like that I could work for hours in the church kitchen preparing to feed the Lord's masses, and just skip my workout for that day. (Or am I confusing recycled with reincarnation?)

I doubt that it was looking out upon this sea of silver hair that caused Bishop Wirz to ask that we be recycled. Like it reminded him of a yard of aluminum cans drained of all the good stuff ? No, it's more like he saw us as good wine—old wine—full bodied wine! Something to be bottled, valued, savored. Christ said, "You can't put new wine into old wine skins." Then He added with a twinkle, "But everyone knows old wine is better!" That's more like it.

Our generation is a dying breed, an endangered species. How many big families do you see today? See what I mean? Today's fertile females found their own remedy for the glitches in the Rhythm Method. I'm not sure what it was, but it certainly shrank families and allowed two careers per household. Now we Seniors do understand you Juniors, so don't worry. (Do we sound like a prom committee?) We understand the two-income family is a reality of the nineties. Without it how can you give the kids the basics in life? And man does not live by bread alone. You've gotta throw in a few pizzas, too. We're proud of our daughters, the new Super Moms.

This does present a problem for the Church, however. Those career women can't step into the roles we played at their age, like officers in parish organizations, newsletter editors, religion teachers, bazaar chairs, and bridge players. The few hours these Moms have at home must be spent on "quality time" with their children. And to make matters worse, convents are empty and big rectories are lucky to have one priest in residence. You can see why we hear this voice crying in the wilderness, "Recycle, recycle!"

Well, worry no more, Bishop, because here we are. Here are your saints who survived the Bootcamp for Sainthood, where we practiced the Spiritual and Corporal Works of Mercy daily, instructing the ignorant, feeding the hungry, clothing the naked. Here are your Master Planners with years of experience as presidents of large, nonprofit organizations (our families).

Here are your Power Houses of Energy ! Where would you like to plug us in?

We type, teach, and toil. We design and decorate. We write, wait, and watch. We cook, clean, compute, bake, barbecue, baby-sit, paint, plant, purchase, pray, serve, stitch, and staple. We even do windows! Don't worry that we look like we're over the hill. We have followed the modern fitness craze, so we may still be able to climb a few more. If our daughters are the Super Moms, I guess we're the Super Duper Moms (duper being the Latin for double duty).

Ours is the first generation of homemakers to have the heavy burdens of housework lifted. We are the beneficiaries of automatic washers, dryers, and dishwashers. We have microwaves to zap and cleaning resources to tap. Like my father said, "Nothing is free in this world." So now we have an answer to our question, What's the catch? The catch is we must do double duty .

So let's hear another chorus of, "Here I am, Lord. I come to do your will. Make of me what pleases you. Here I am, here I am, Lord !"

And don't forget the overtime in my paycheck.

ORDER FORM

Please send ———— copies of *Grand Mom, Growing Old Gracefully & Other Likely Stories* by Audrey Mettel Fixmer

Ship to:

_____
(print name)

_____
(post office box or street address, apartment number)

_____
(city, state, zip)

I enclose $8.00 for each book ordered ————————
    plus $1.50 postage and handling for
    the first book and .75 for each
    additional book ordered ————————
    Wis. residents, add 5.5% tax ————————
TOTAL AMOUNT ENCLOSED ————————

Send only check or money order to:
        Write-On-Time Publishing Company
        P.O. Box 216
        Fort Atkinson, WI 53538

Please allow 3 weeks for delivery.